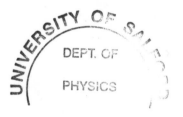

BASIC materials studies

Butterworths BASIC Series includes the following titles:

BASIC aerodynamics
BASIC hydraulics
BASIC hydrology
BASIC materials studies
BASIC matrix methods
BASIC mechanical vibrations
BASIC numerical mathematics
BASIC soil mechanics
BASIC statistics
BASIC stress analysis
BASIC thermodynamics and heat transfer

BASIC materials studies

P N Peapell, MSc, MIM, CEng
Principal Lecturer, Materials Technology Group,
Royal Military College of Science, Shrivenham, England

and

J A Belk, BSc, PhD, FIM, CEng
Professor and Head of Materials Technology,
Royal Military College of Science, Shrivenham, England

Butterworths
London . Boston . Durban . Singapore . Sydney . Toronto . Wellington

First published 1985

© Butterworth & Co. (Publishers) Ltd 1985

British Library Cataloguing in Publication Data

Peapell, P. N.
  BASIC materials studies.
  1. Materials—Data processing   2. Solids
  —Data processing   3. Basic (Computer
  program language)
  I. Title   II. Belk, J. A.
  620.1'1'0287   TA403

  ISBN 0-408-01374-5

Library of Congress Cataloging in Publication Data

Peapell, P. N.
  BASIC materials studies.

  Includes bibliographies and index.
  1. Materials—Data processing.   2. Basic (Computer
  program language) I. Belk, J. A.
  II. Title. III. Title: B.A.S.I.C. materials studies.
  TA407.P33   1985   620.1'1   84-19983
  ISBN 0-408-01374-5

Typeset by Illustrated Arts Limited, Sutton, Surrey
Printed and bound by Thomson Litho Ltd., East Kilbride, Scotland.

Preface

This book is intended to be used as a supplement to a variety of materials courses rather than a textbook for a specific material course, hence the topics chosen are illustrative rather than comprehensive. It should be of interest to students engaged on a variety of vocational and non-vocational materials courses of up to undergraduate level. Our intention has been to indicate to students how simple computer programs can be used to illustrate and clarify materials principles and to encourage students to write their own programs to solve problems not contained in this text.

The great majority of programs used employ the smallest BASIC vocabulary of commands and no multi-statement lines. Hence students with only a brief introduction to BASIC will be able to use the book, and the programs should easily transfer for use on any computer employing one of the many dialects of BASIC. The computer used to develop the programs cannot handle string arrays; however, it is shown in Chapter 6 that this is not a significant restriction and alternative listings using string arrays are illustrated. In contrast to other books in this series we have used graphical display to illustrate the results of some of the programs. Necessarily the graphics commands are specific to the Tektronix computer used but their definitions are given in Chapter 1 and so the programs can be readily modified for computers with other graphics systems.

The order of the chapters and the material within each chapter has been chosen to provide a progression from a materials viewpoint rather than a progressive increase in programming complexity. Students with little or no experience of computing are recommended to select the sections of the chapters with the simpler programs first and progress with more complex programs later.

Although we recognize that failure of materials is an important aspect of any materials course, we have not included any programs on this topic, as to include these would have meant omitting topics from the other chapters and the complexity of some of the phenomena, for instance creep, make the programs longer and more suitable for a more advanced treatment.

We wish to acknowledge assistance from many of our colleagues at RMSC, particularly Dr M R Edwards for his critical appraisal of the manuscript.

P N Peapell
J A Belk
Shrivenham 1984

For

Katharine *and* Maureen

Contents

Preface

1   Introduction to BASIC   **1**

1.1 The BASIC approach   1
1.2 The elements of BASIC   1
1.3 Checking programs   8
1.4 Different computers and variants of BASIC   8
1.5 Graphics commands   9
1.6 Special commands   10
Bibliography   10

2   Structure of materials   **11**

ESSENTIAL THEORY   11

2.1 Introduction   11
2.2 Atoms on crystal planes   12
2.3 Dislocations   14
2.4 Stereographic projection   17
2.5 Atomic and weight percent   18
2.6 Hume–Rothery primary solid solubility rules   18
2.7 Binary eutectic equilibrium diagram   20
2.8 Coring in a binary alloy   21
2.9 Quantitative metallography   22

PROGRAMS   25

2.1 Atoms on a crystal plane   25
2.2 Dislocations   28
2.3 Stereographic projection   30
2.4 Atomic and weight percent compositions   33
2.5 Hume–Rothery primary solid solubility   34
2.6 Binary eutectic equilibrium diagram   36
2.7 Coring   40
2.8 Quantitative metallography   41

PROBLEMS   43

References   48
Bibliography   48

3 Thermodynamics and kinetics of solids   **49**

ESSENTIAL THEORY   49

3.1 Introduction   49
3.2 Thermodynamic relationships   50
3.3 Rates of reaction — the Arrhenius equation   51
3.4 Diffusion   52
3.5 Analysis of resistivity data   53
3.6 Shear transformation (martensitic reactions)   55
3.7 Corrosion   56

PROGRAMS   59

3.1 Calculation of activation energy — diffusion of
     Cu in CuO   59
3.2 Calculation of reaction times from activation energy   64
3.3 Calculation of diffusion profiles — Fick's second law   65
3.4 Analysis of resistivity data: Johnson–Mehl   67
3.5 Determination of hardenability   70
3.6 Corrosion — calculation of cell voltages   74

PROBLEMS   75

References   76
Bibliography   76

4 Mechanical properties of polymers   **77**

ESSENTIAL THEORY   77

4.1 Introduction   77
4.2 Degree of polymerization   77
4.3 Average molecular weights   78
4.4 Elastic strain and elastic energy stored   79
4.5 Work done in deformation   80
4.6 Stress or strain relaxation   80
4.7 Viscoelastic modulus   81
4.8 Elastomer stress–strain curve   83
4.9 Molecular weight and strength of polystyrene   84

PROGRAMS   84

4.1 Degree of polymerization   84
4.2 Weight and number average molecular weights   85
4.3 Elastic strain and energy   87
4.4 Work done in deformation   87
4.5 Anelastic relaxation time   88
4.6 Viscoelastic modulus   89
4.7 Elastomer stress–strain   91

4.8 Molecular weight and tensile compact strength   92

PROBLEMS   92

Reference   96
Bibliography   96

5 Deformation and strength of crystalline materials   **97**

ESSENTIAL THEORY   97

5.1 Introduction   97
5.2 Theoretical strength   97
5.3 Deformation of single crystals — critical resolved
    shear stress   99
5.4 Tensile deformation of polycrystalline materials   100
5.5 Three-point bend testing   104
5.6 Hardness   105

PROGRAMS   106

5.1 Critical resolved shear stress   106
5.2 Tensile analysis   108
5.3 Yield point phenomena   113
5.4 Neutral axis and inter-laminar shear stress (ILSS)   115
5.5 Hardness Vickers–ocular to H_v conversion   117

PROBLEMS   119

References   121
Bibliography   121

6 Materials properties comparisons   **122**

ESSENTIAL THEORY   122

6.1 Introduction   122
6.2 Order of merit classification   125
6.3 The data   126

PROGRAM   128

PROBLEMS   137

Reference   137
Bibliography   138

Index   139

Chapter 1

Introduction to BASIC

1.1 The BASIC approach

The programs in this book are written in BASIC (Beginners All-purpose Symbolic Instruction Code) which was developed at Dartmouth College, USA as an easy-to-learn general purpose programming language. Originally intended for use on time-sharing computer systems, it has gained widespread popularity as the main language for microcomputers, being not only easy to learn, but also easy to use. It is very simple to write a program, type it into the computer, run it and correct any errors and then run it again to obtain the required output in a short time.

The main criticisms of simple BASIC relate to its lack of structure (see Section 1.4) but this is unimportant for the short programs presented in the following chapters.

This book is not an instruction manual on BASIC, but it does aim to help to learn BASIC by applying it to a relevant engineering subject through studying the examples and perhaps copying them and running them with different data and inputs and then trying some of the problems.

Although not a BASIC manual, a short description of the grammar of simple BASIC is given below to help the reader clarify any language problem.

1.2 The elements of BASIC

1.2.1 Mathematical expressions

One of the main objects of the example programs in this book is to evaluate and operate on the equations that arise in materials studies.

These equations contain numerical constants and variables (e.g. x) and functions (e.g. sin). All numbers are treated identically whether they be integers (e.g. 36) or real (e.g. 36.1). An exponential form is used to represent large or small numbers (e.g. 3.61 E6 represents 3.61×10^6). Numeric variables are represented by a letter or a letter followed by a digit (e.g. E or E1). On many computers π is directly available to the user either as PI or as a π key. (In this book PI has been used.) An operation such as a square root can be done by using an in-built function (e.g. SQR(X)). The argument in brackets (X) can be a number, a variable or a mathematical expression. For trigonometrical functions (SIN(X), COS(X), etc.) the argument is interpreted in radians. Other functions include a natural logarithm and its exponential (LOG and EXP respectively), ABS which selects the absolute value of the argument and INT which selects the integral part of the argument.

Mathematical equations also contain operations such as plus, minus, etc. These operators have a hierarchy in that some are performed by the computer before others. In descending order of hierarchy the operators are

to the power of ( )
multiply (*) and divide (/)
add (+) and subtract (−).

Thus, for example, multiplication is carried out before addition. The computer works from left to right in an expression if the operators have the same hierarchy. The use of brackets allows any of these operations to be overridden. Hence $\dfrac{a+b}{3c}$ becomes (A + B)/(3*C) or (A + B)/B/C.

1.2.2 Program structure and assignment

A BASIC program is a sequence of statements which define a procedure for the computer to follow. As it follows this procedure the computer allocates values to each of the variables. The values of some of these variables may be specified by data that are input to the program. Others are generated in the program using, for instance, the assignment statement. This has the form

line number |LET| variable = mathematical expression

where the word LET is usually optional and therefore omitted. As an example, the root of quadratic equation

$$x_1 = \frac{-b + \sqrt{b^2 - 4ac}}{2a}$$

may be obtained from a statement such as

100 X1 = (−B + SQR(B^2 − 4*A*C))/(2*A)

It is important to realize that an assignment statement is not itself an equation. Rather, it is an instruction to the computer to give the variable on the left-hand side the numeric value of the expression on the right-hand side. It is therefore possible to have a statement

    50 X = X + 1

which increases by 1 the value of X. Each variable can have only one value at any time unless it is subscripted (see Section 1.2.7).

Note that all BASIC statements (i.e. all program lines) are numbered. The line number defines the order in which such statements are executed.

1.2.3 Input

For interactive or 'conversational' programs the user specifies variables by inputting data in response to prompts from the computer as the program is running. The statement has the form

    line number INPUT variable 1 [, variable 2, . . .]

e.g. 20 INPUT A, B, C.

When the program is run the computer prints ? as it reaches this statement and waits for the user to type values for the variables, e.g.

    ? 5, 10, 15

which makes A = 5, B = 10 and C = 15 in the example above.

An alternative form of data input is useful if there are many data or if the data are not to be changed by the user. For this type of data specification there is a statement of the form

    line number READ variable 1 [, variable 2, . . .]

e.g.

    20 READ A, B, C

with an associated statement (or number of statements) of the form

    line number DATA number 1 [, number 2, . . .]

e.g.

    1 DATA 5, 10, 15

or

    1 DATA 5
    2 DATA 10
    3 DATA 15

DATA statements can be placed anywhere in a program — it is often convenient to place them at the beginning of the program so that they can be easily changed.

When using built-in data it is sometimes necessary to read data from their start more than once during a single program run. This is done using the statement

> line number RESTORE

1.2.4 Output

Output of the data and the results of calculations, etc. is implemented by using a statement of the form

> line number PRINT list

where the list may contain variables or expressions, e.g.

> 200 PRINT A,B,C A*B/C

text enclosed in quotes, e.g.

> 10 PRINT "INPUT A,B,C IN MM"

or mixed text and variables, e.g.

> 300 PRINT "PRESSURE IS"; P; "N/NM ˆ 2".

The items in the list are separated by commas or semicolons. Commas give tabulations in columns, each about 15 spaces wide, while a semicolon suppresses this spacing. If a semicolon is placed at the end of a list it has the function of suppressing the line feed. If the list is left empty a blank line is printed.

The necessity of using PRINT statements in association with both 'run-time' input (to indicate what input is required) and READ/ DATA statements (because otherwise the program user has no record of the data) should be noted.

1.2.5 Conditional statements

It is often necessary to enable a program to take some action if, and only if, some condition is fulfilled. This is done with a statement of the form

> line number IF expression 1 conditional operator expression 2 THEN line number

where the possible conditional operators are

> = equals
> <> not equal to
> < less than
> < = less than or equal to
> > greater then
> > = greater than or equal to

For example, a program could contain the following statements if it is to stop when a zero value of A is input

```
20 INPUT A
30 IF A <>0 THEN 50
40 STOP
50 . . .
```

In this example, note the statement

line number STOP

which stops the run of a program. The statement

line number END

may be used at the end of a program though this is not essential.

1.2.6 Loops

There are several means by which a program can repeat some of its procedure. The simplest such statement is

line number GO TO line number

This statement could be used with the conditional statement example above so that the program continues to request values of A until the user inputs zero.

The most common way of performing loops is with a starting statement of the form

line number FOR variables = expression 1 TO expression 2 [STEP expression 3]

where the step is assumed to be unity if omitted. The finish of the loop is signified by a statement

line number NEXT variable

where the same variable is used in both FOR and NEXT statements. Its value should not be changed in the intervening lines.

A loop is used if, for example, N sets of data have to be READ and their reciprocals printed, e.g.

```
10 READ N
20 PRINT "NUMBER", "RECIPROCAL"
30 FOR I = 1 TO N
40 READ A
50 PRINT A, 1/A
60 NEXT I
```

Loops can also be used to generate data. Consider the example (given below) of a simple temperature conversion program

```
10 PRINT "CENTIGRADE", "FAHRENHEIT"
20 FOR C = 0 to 100 STEP 5
30 PRINT C, 9*C/5 + 32
40 NEXT C
```

1.2.7 Subscripted variables

It is sometimes very convenient to allow a single variable to have a number of different values during a single program run. For instance, if a program contains data for several different forces on a specimen it is convenient for these to be called $Q(1)$, $Q(2)$, $Q(3)$, etc. instead of Q1, Q2, Q3, etc. It is then possible for a single statement to perform calculations for all the forces, e.g.

```
50 FOR I = 1 TO N
60 V(I) = Q(1)/A
70 NEXT I
```

which determines the stress in the specimen (which is of cross-sectional area A) for each force.

A non-subscripted variable has a single value associated with it and if a subscripted variable is used it is necessary to provide space for all the values. This is done with a dimensioning statement of the form

line number DIM variable 1 (integer 1) [, variable 2 (integer 2). . . .]

e.g.

```
20 DIM V(20), Q(20)
```

which allows up to 20 values of V and Q. The DIM statement must occur before the subscripted variables are first used.

On some computers it is possible to use a dimension statement of a different form, e.g.

```
20 DIM V(N), Q(N)
```

where the value of N has been previously defined. This form, when available, has the advantage of not wasting storage space.

1.2.8 Sub-routines

Sometimes a sequence of statements needs to be accessed more than once in the same program. Instead of merely repeating these statements it is better to put them in a sub-routine. The program then contains statements of the form

line number GOSUB line number

When the program reaches this statement it branches (i.e. transfers control) to the second line number. The sequence of statements starting with this second line number ends with a statement

line number RETURN

and the program returns control to the statement immediately after the GOSUB call.

Sub-routines can be placed anywhere in the program but it is usually convenient to position them at the end separate from the main program statements.

Another reason for using a sub-routine occurs when a procedure is written which is required in more than one program. In sub-routines it is sometimes desirable to use less common variable names (e.g. X9 instead of X) so that the possibility of the same variable name being used with a different meaning in separate parts of the program is minimized.

1.2.9 Other statements

(1) Explanatory remarks or headings which are not to be output can be inserted into a program using

line number REM comment

Any statement beginning with the word REM is ignored by the computer. On some computers it is possible to include remarks on the same line as other statements.

(2) Non-numeric data (e.g. words) can be handled by string variables. A string is a series of characters within quotes (e.g. "PRESSURE") and a string variable is a letter followed by a $ sign (e.g. A$). String variables are particularly valuable when printed headings need to be changed.

(3) Multiple branching can be done with statements of the form

line number ON expression THEN line number 1 [, line number 2, . . .]

and

line number ON expression GOSUB line number 1 [, line number 2, . . .]

When a program reaches one of these statements it branches to line number 1 if the integer value of the expression is 1, to line number 2 if the expression is 2, and so on. An error message is printed if the expression gives a value less than or greater than the number of referenced line numbers.

(4) Functions other than those built into the language such as $SIN(X)$, etc. can be created by using a DEF statement. For example

10 DEF FNA(X) = X^3 + X^2

defines a cubic function which can be recalled later in the program as FNA (variable) where the value of this variable is substituted for X. A defined function is of use where an algebraic expression is to be evaluated several times in a program.

(These last two statement forms have not been used in this book.)

1.3 Checking programs

Most computers give a clear indication if there are grammatical (syntax) errors in a BASIC program. Program statements can be modified by retyping them completely or by using special editing procedures. The majority of syntax errors are easy to locate but if a variable has been used with two (or more) different meanings in separate parts of the program some 'mystifying' errors can result.

It is not sufficient for the program to be just grammatically correct — it must also give the correct answers. A program should therefore be checked either by using data which give a known solution, or by hand calculation.

If the program is to be used with a wide range of data or by users other than the program writer, it is necessary to check that all parts of it function. It is also important to ensure that the program does not give incorrect, yet plausible, answers when 'nonsense' data are input. It is quite difficult to make programs completely 'userproof' and they become somewhat lengthy by so doing. The programs in this book have been kept as short as possible for the purpose of clarity and may not therefore be fully 'userproof'.

1.4 Different computers and variants of BASIC

The examples in this book use a simple version of BASIC that should work on most computers, even those with small storage capacity. Only single line statements have been used though many computers allow a number of statements on each line with a separator such as \. Multiple assignments may also be possible so that, for instance, one may write a single statement such as

$$1000\ A(0) = B(0) = C(0) = D(0) = 0$$

There is one important feature which distinguishes computers, particularly microcomputers with visual display units (VDUs). This concerns the number of columns available across each line and the number of lines that are visible on the screen. Simple modifications to some of the example programs may be necessary to fit the output to a particular microcomputer. TAB printing is a useful facility for this purpose.

Various enhancements of BASIC have been made since its inception – these have been implemented on a number of computer systems. The programs in this book could be rewritten to take account of some of these 'advanced' features. For example, the ability to use long variable names (e.g. VELOCITY instead of say V or VI) makes it easier to write unambiguous programs. Other advanced facilities include more powerful looping and conditional statements and independent sub-routines which make structured programs easier to write. Expressed simply, structured programming involves the compartmentalization of programs and minimizes branching resulting from statements containing 'GOTO line number' and 'THEN line number'. Good program structure is advantageous in long programs.

1.5 Graphics commands

The commands listed below are specific to the Tektronix 4051 system but should work with little modification on other systems.

VIEWPORT   The viewport is defined as the drawing surface upon which graphics data are plotted. The VIEWPORT statement establishes the boundaries of the drawing surface on the VDU or on an external peripheral device. The surface may be any rectangular shape and can be located anywhere on the screen. For the 4051 system the ranges are 0–130 (x-axis) and 0–100 (y-axis). The values are in graphic display units (GDUs), e.g.

VIEWPORT   0,   80,   0,   100
x min, x max, y min, y max

WINDOW   The window is an image of the viewport cast on to the user data space. The WINDOW statement specifies what portion of the data fits into the viewport and allows the coordinates of different points on the screen to be specified in user data units, e.g.

WINDOW   0,   10,   0,   5000
x min, x max, y min, y max

SCALE   The SCALE statement specifies how many user data units fit inside a GDU. Although this ratio can obviously be set with the WINDOW and VIEWPORT statements, the SCALE statement provides a quick and easy way to establish the ratio, e.g.

SCALE   10/80   5000/100
             Horizontal   Vertical scale
             scale factor   factor

AXIS   The AXIS statement causes the BASIC interpreter to draw an X–Y axis on the VDU. The intercept point can be specified anywhere on the screen and the interval between tick marks on the axes can be specified to be any distance, e.g.

AXIS	0, 0,	1, 100
	Origin	x and y
	coordinates	tick intervals

MOVE X,Y   Moves the graphic point to the absolute coordinates X,Y, e.g.

MOVE X,Y

RMOVE X, Y   Moves the graphic point on the VDU to a position X units horizontally and Y units vertically from its present position.

DRAW X,Y   Draws a line from the current position of the graphic point to the coordinates X,Y.

RDRAW X,Y   Draws a line to a position which is X units horizontally and Y units vertically from the current position of the graphic pointer.

1.6 Special commands

Some computers have special 'built-in' routines or routines which may be added via 'firmware' packs. One of these commands is utilized in Program 5.2. CALL 'Max' — this command will return the maximum value in a specified array and the position of the maximum. Whilst this command can be seen to be very useful its function may readily be duplicated by a simple user written routine, see lines 3230 to 3340 of Program 6.1.

Bibliography

The books noted below represent only a fraction of those available on BASIC programming.

Kemeny, J. G. and Kurtz, T. E., *BASIC Programming*, John Wiley, (1968).

Monro, D. M., *Interactive Computing with BASIC*, Edward Arnold, (1974).

Gottfried, B. S., *Programming with BASIC*, Schaum's Outline Series, McGraw-Hill, (1975).

Alcock, D. *Illustrating BASIC*, Cambridge University Press, (1977).

Forsyth, R. *The BASIC Idea*, Chapman & Hall, (1978).

Chapter 2

Structure of materials

ESSENTIAL THEORY

2.1 Introduction

Three aspects of the structure of materials are covered in this chapter. First, the arrangement of atoms in crystals; secondly the composition and quantity of phases within the structure and thirdly the microscopical assessment of the distribution of phases in a structure. The programs covering atomic arrangements deal only with crystalline materials, as the regularity of structure enables simple programs to be used. The arrangement of atoms in the crystal is crucial to the properties of the material and the arrangement of atoms on particular crystal planes governs the deformation properties of the crystal. Hence the first section concerns the graphical representation of atomic arrangements in crystals. Crystal structure is also important and this is determined by diffraction techniques. The same analysis can be used to interpret the diffraction patterns which arise from common cubic crystals by utilizing the concept of the reciprocal lattice. Real crystals are not perfect but contain various types of defect. The imperfections which have the largest influence on mechanical properties are the line defects known as dislocations and the second section deals briefly with the strains and forces around and between elementary dislocations. As an aid to plotting three-dimensional relationships between planes and directions in crystals, the stereographic projection is very valuable. The third section deals with the way in which a cubic crystal can be simply represented by a two-dimensional plot on the stereographic projection.

The second important area of materials structure concerns the composition of phases that are present within a structure. Composition can be expressed as atomic or weight percent and Program 2.1 deals with the conversion of one type of compositional data to another. Solid solutions are fundamental to all common alloys and the ability of one element to form a solid solution with another is basic to much of alloy design. Program 2.2 deals with the Hume–Rothery rules for primary solubility and indicates the likelihood of extensive solid solution occurring between given elements. The interpretation of equilibrium phase diagrams is not always easily grasped and an interactive computer program can be of considerable assistance. It can indicate which phases are present in an alloy of given composition at a given temperature, what their compositions are and in what proportion each of the phases is present. Since this information is so readily available, the effect of changes in either composition or temperature around and across phase boundaries can easily be appreciated. The previous program deals only with phases present in alloys under equilibrium conditions, but segregation of alloying elements occurs in the great majority of cast materials. The final program in this section of the chapter deals with the segregation of alloy elements within the grains of a cast alloy, which is often known as coring. Some simple assumptions are made on the basis of which the variation of composition and the presence of second phase in a typical chill cast alloy can be estimated.

The final section of the chapter deals with the analysis of the microstructure of a material which results from its processing route. The microstructure may be single phase and so consist of grains of one material only, or it may be two phase, in which case it can usually be characterized as particles in a matrix. These two basic microstructures are considered and the quantitative information which is available from analysis of the microstructure is indicated by a relatively simple program.

2.2 Atoms on crystal planes

Discussions of the way in which crystals deform, be it by slip or by twinning, are often centred on the distribution of atoms on particular crystal planes (see Chapter 5). For instance the close-packed planes are normally the slip planes. Also the directions within those planes are specific to the deformation mechanisms and slip takes place normally along the close-packed directions. For these reasons it is useful to be able to inspect standard simple crystal structures and determine what the distribution of atoms is on any particular plane. Simple planes can be visualized and the distribution of atoms calculated by hand, but higher order planes lead to much more difficulty both of visualization and calculation. For example, a unit cube of a body centred and face centred crystal are illustrated in Figure 2.1. The position of the (110) plane is shown in each cube and the arrangement of atoms on those planes is indicated below. It is simple to calculate the atomic positions in this case but the arrangement of atoms on higher order planes can only be determined by intersecting a larger number of unit cubes and the analysis soon becomes tedious and confusing if done by hand. The computer can

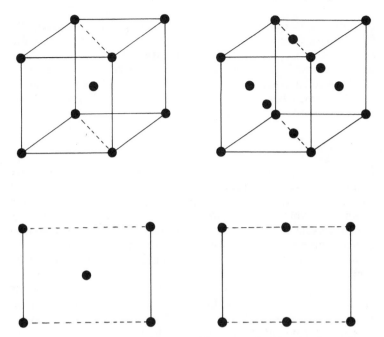

Figure 2.1 Atoms in body-centred and face-centred-cubic unit cubes and
their distribution on the (110) plane

perform this function for an element of crystal containing a substantial number of unit cubes and produce a simple graphical result.

Apart from the use of such a scheme for noting the atomic distributon on slip, twin and growth planes of crystals, it also has great value in the interpretation of diffraction patterns, through the use of the reciprocal lattice concept. For every real crystal one can construct a reciprocal lattice of points each of which represents a diffracting plane in the real crystal. The reciprocal lattice whose unit cell is defined by the vectors $\mathbf{b}_1$, $\mathbf{b}_2$ and $\mathbf{b}_3$ can be derived from a crystal whose unit cell is defined by the vectors $\mathbf{a}_1$, $\mathbf{a}_2$ and $\mathbf{a}_3$ by the equations

$$\mathbf{b}_1 = \tfrac{1}{V}\,(\mathbf{a}_2 \times \mathbf{a}_3)$$
$$\mathbf{b}_2 = \tfrac{1}{V}\,(\mathbf{a}_3 \times \mathbf{a}_1)$$
$$\mathbf{b}_3 = \tfrac{1}{V}\,(\mathbf{a}_1 \times \mathbf{a}_2)$$

where V = volume of the unit cell of the crystal. Since every point in the reciprocal lattice represents a diffracting plane in the real crystal a plane section through the reciprocal lattice at right angles to a given direction produces a planar array of points whose positions correspond to the electron diffraction pattern obtained from the crystal with an electron beam incident along the given direction. Since a real face centred cubic crystal has a body centred cubic reciprocal lattice, all diffraction patterns from a face centred cubic crystal may be found by sectioning a body centred cubic reciprocal lattice. Similarly a body centred cubic crystal has a face centred cubic reciprocal lattice so again all electron diffraction patterns can easily be found.

2.3 Dislocations

The elementary concepts of edge and screw dislocations are fairly easy to appreciate, but students often fail to recognize the important differences between these two types of dislocation in respect to the strain fields which surround them or the forces between them.

Real crystals contain imperfections which affect their properties. An atom missing from a lattice site or a foreign atom on a lattice site is known as a point defect. The defect that has the most influence on plastic deformation is a line defect known as a dislocation. Consider a block of perfect crystal as shown in Figure 2.2(a). The bonds across the plane ABCD can be broken and one part of the crystal given a shear of one lattice vector and then the bonds reformed. If the shear is in the direction BA we obtain the block shown in Figure 2.2(b) which now includes an edge dislocation, whereas if the shear is in the direction BC we obtain the block shown in Figure 2.2(c) which includes a screw dislocation. In both cases the dislocation line is AD and the dislocation marks off the part of the crystal plane that has sheared from that which has not. Both types of dislocation can move through the crystal under the influence of a shear stress much below that required to permanently deform a perfect crystal (see Chapter 5).

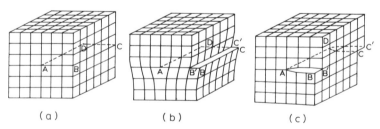

(a)   (b)   (c)

Figure 2.2 A block of perfect crystal (a) sheared to form (b) an edge dislocation and (c) a screw dislocation

As the dislocation moves, an equal number of bonds are made and broken and the area of crystal that has sheared is increased. A dislocation cannot terminate within a crystal but its direction in the crystal can change. A dislocation is characterized by the unit lattice vector through which the respective parts of the crystal are sheared, in Figure 2.2(b) and (c) this is BB′. This is known as the Burgers vector **b** and is perpendicular to the dislocation line for an edge dislocation and parallel to the dislocation line for a screw dislocation. If the direction of a dislocation line changes in the slip plane the Burgers vector remains in a constant direction so the dislocation changes its type. If an edge dislocation line bends through 90° on the slip plane it becomes a screw dislocation and vice versa. It will be clear that the general dislocation has mixed screw and edge components but it is simple to consider the two elementary types initially at least.

If an equal sided square path is traced around the dislocation on the front face of Figure 2.2(c) the finishing point is exactly one Burgers vector above or below the starting point. The crystal planes are distorted into the form of a spiral staircase. Clearly the strain is equal at all points around the axis of the dislocation but increases considerably as the core of the dislocation is approached. The shear strain ϕ surrounding a screw dislocation is given by the formula

$$\phi = \mathbf{b}/2\pi R$$

where **b** is the Burgers vector of the dislocation and R is the distance from the dislocation. There is no other strain associated with a screw dislocation but an edge dislocation has compressive and dilatational strain also. The above formula for shear strain also applies to the edge dislocation but there is an additional strain given by the formula

$$\delta = \frac{\mathbf{b}}{2\pi R}\frac{1 - 2\nu}{1 - \nu}\sin\theta$$

where R and θ are polar coordinates, and ν Poisson's ratio. δ is clearly negative if $180° > \theta > 0°$ and positive if $360° > \theta > 180°$. It is also zero at 0° and 180° and has its maximum positive and negative values at 270° and 90° respectively. A glance at Figure 2.2(b) will show that the top half of the crystal has been compressed and the lower half extended confirming the above formula.

As each dislocation has an associated strain field it will obviously be affected by the presence of another dislocation nearby. Like dislocations on the same slip plane repel each other, but the situation is not so simple for like dislocations on parallel slip planes. The force between two screw dislocations is parallel to the line joining the cores of the two dislocations. Hence there is always a component in the slip plane tending to drive the two dislocations apart along their respective slip planes. The situation is different for two edge dislocations on parallel slip planes. If the second dislocation is further away along the slip plane than it is perpendicular to the slip plane there is a net repulsive force along the slip plane. If, however, the second dislocation is closer along the slip plane than it is perpendicular to the slip plane there is an attractive force tending to bring the second dislocation into line above the first. This leads to the formation of so-called tilt boundaries where a parallel set of like edge dislocations act like a series of fence posts marking off two areas of crystal with slight misorientations.

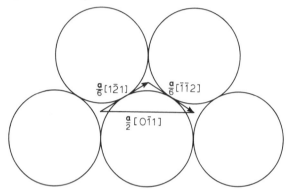

Figure 2.3 Combination of Burger's vectors from two partial dislocations to form the Burger's vector of a unit dislocation

The energy of a dislocation is proportional to the square of the Burgers vector. Figure 2.3 indicates that the Burgers vector **a**/2[011] of a unit dislocation in the (111) slip plane of a face centred cubic crystal can be replaced by two partial dislocations with Burgers vectors **a**/6[121] and **a**/6[112]. The dissociation of a unit dislocation into two partials is energetically favourable as $a^2/2$ is greater than $a^2/6 + a^2/6$. However, if a unit dislocation does dissociate, the two partial dislocations move apart and are joined by a ribbon of faulted material known as a stacking fault. If the stacking fault energy per unit area is γ the equilibrium separation of two such partial dislocations can be shown to be

$$d = \frac{\mu a^2}{24\pi\gamma}$$

where a = lattice parameter and u = modulus of rigidity.

Stacking fault energies vary from 0.04 J/m^2 to 0.2 J/m^2 for common metallic elements. Alloy additions are made to creep resisting alloys to lower the stacking fault energy and so enable the partial dislocations to move further apart.

2.4 Stereographic projection

The stereographic projection is a very versatile and valuable way of plotting three-dimensional information on two dimensions. In crystallography, it is widely used to illustrate the three-dimensional relationships between planes and directions, to make measurements between directions and to perform operations such as rotation about a particular axis. The crystal is considered to be at the centre of a hemisphere and the normals or poles of crystallographic planes are extended to cut the hemisphere as shown in Figure 2.4.

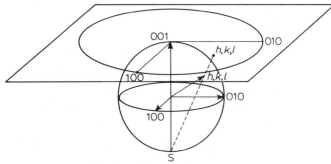

Figure 2.4 Schematic diagram of the formation of the stereographic projection

Their positions on the hemisphere are now projected on to the plane tangential to the top point of the hemisphere from the bottom point S of the sphere of which the hemisphere is the top half. Thus every pole or direction in three-dimensional space can be represented by a point on a circular plot or special projection. The stereographic projection has many unique attributes which are discussed at length in the references given later but, as it is so widely used in crystallography, the ability to plot the pole of the plane (h,k,l) quickly and accurately is valuable.

The method of plotting is illustrated in Figures 2.5 and 2.6. In Figure 2.5 the standard 001 projection is shown with the (h,k,l) pole

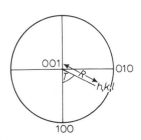

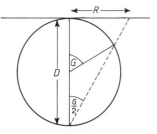

Figure 2.5 Polar coordinates used in plotting stereographic projection

Figure 2.6 Diagram illustrating the relationship of R to the pole (h,k,l)

indicated. Its polar coordinates are R and T. The angle T is the angle between the $(h,k,0)$ pole and the (100) pole is given by $\tan^{-1}(k/h)$, and the origin of R is shown on Figure 2.6. The pole (h,k,l) makes angle G with the (001) pole where $\cos G = \dfrac{l}{\sqrt{h^2 + k^2 + l^2}}$ $R = D \tan$ $(G/2)$, where D is the diameter of the sphere, which becomes the radius of the projection. The program described allows any value of (h,k,l) to be plotted. If l is negative the pole will not intersect the top hemisphere in Figure 2.4, but the bottom one. In this case the pole $(\bar{h},\bar{k},\bar{l})$ does intersect the top hemisphere so this is plotted.

2.5 Atomic and weight percent

The composition of an alloy or of the phases in an alloy is very important in determining its properties. However, one can define composition either as the percentage of atoms of one sort or another, or as the percentage of weight of one element or another. As all elements have different atomic weights, the 'atomic percent' and 'weight percent' compositions are often quite different. Although for brass 30 wt % Zn is 29.41 at % because copper and zinc have similar atomic weights, 4 wt % Cu in Al is 1.74 at % and 0.8 wt % C in Fe is 3.62 at %, so some means of conversion is important.

The conversion of atomic percent compositions into weight percent compositions and vice versa is mathematically a comparatively simple undertaking for two elements. A circular slide rule is available which allows this conversion to be done. The situation becomes more complicated and time consuming when more than two elements are present as the slide rule cannot be used. The computer program for this conversion is almost as simple for ten elements as it is for two elements, so it is an ideal illustration of the use of a simple computer program to perform a useful operation. The formulae used are stated below, the denominators being the sums over all elements that are present in the alloy.

$$A_A = \frac{C_A/W_A}{\Sigma C_I/W_I}$$

$$C_A = \frac{A_A W_A}{\Sigma A_I W_I}$$

where C_A = weight percent of A, A_A = atomic percent of A and W_A = atomic weight of A.

2.6 Hume–Rothery primary solid solubility rules

Hume–Rothery's rules for primary solid solubility, which were originally formulated for the mono-valent, non-transition metals, make a useful illustration of the use of computing to elementary alloy theory. Hume–Rothery pointed out that the important parameters of an atom, as far as primary solubility was concerned, were its atomic radius, the number of valency electrons and its electro-negativity. The greater the size difference between the solute and solvent atoms, the more restricted will be the solid solubility. In particular a difference in atomic radii of more than 14 percent is unfavourable and solid solubility will be small. This applies to substitutional solid solutions because the presence of a foreign atom that is of significantly different size from the matrix atoms will impose a strain on the lattice. Only a limited amount of strain can be accommodated overall so the greater the size difference the smaller the solubility. Some atoms, such as metals, can easily be freed of an electron or two and become positive ions. These elements are known as electro-positive elements. Other elements such as the halogens, oxygen and sulphur will readily accept an electron to become a negative ion. These elements are known as electro-negative elements.

Some method is necessary to measure the extent to which a particular element is electro-negative or electro-positive, and we use here the so-called electro-negativity scale first proposed by Pauling and modified later by Pritchard and Skinner[1]. Table 2.1 lists

Table 2.1 Electro-negativity scale[1]

Fe	3.9	Ag, Cu	1.7
0	3.5	Ga, Ti	1.6
N, Cl	3.0	Al, In, Zn, Zr	1.5
Br	2.8	Be, Cd, Tl	1.4
C, S, I	2.5	Sc, Y	1.3
Se	2.4	Mg	1.2
Au, H, P, Te	2.1	Ca, Li, Sr	1.0
As, B	2.0	Ba, Na	0.9
Hg, Sb	1.9	K, Rb	0.8
Bi, Ge, Pb, Si, Sn	1.8	Cs	0.7

the elements and their electro-negativity values. These are applied by subtracting one from the other, whereupon the resulting value determines the extent to which the bond between unlike atoms is an ionic bond. If the difference in the electro-negativity numbers is low, only a small proportion of the bond is ionic and if the difference between the electro-negativities is large, a substantial part of the bond is of ionic character. A largely ionic bond between two elements means that the primary solubility will be reduced and the criterion for judgement is built into the program.

For alloys of copper, silver and gold particularly the element of low valency will dissolve more of the element of higher valency than vice versa. For these alloys the limit of primary solubility is dependent on the valency of the solute. The maximum solubility occurs when the electron to atom ratio is 1:4. Thus if Zn, which has two valency electrons, is added to Cu which has only one the maximum solubility C is such that

$$2 \times C + 1\,(1 - C) = 1.4$$

Therefore

$$C = 1.4 - 1 = 0.4 \text{ or } 40\%$$

This calculation is included for those alloys for which it is valid.

2.7 Binary eutectic equilibrium diagram

Newcomers to the study of equilibrium diagrams often find them confusing for a number of reasons. There is no obvious distinction between single- and two-phase fields and the information which is contained within the diagram is often difficult for the student to extract. This information covers the number of phases present at any given position within the diagram and their names, but also the proportions of the two phases and the compositions of those phases.

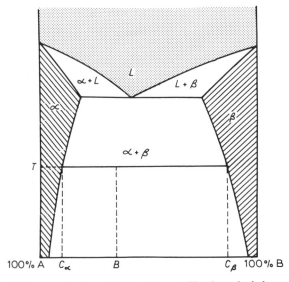

Figure 2.7 Binary eutectic equilibrium diagram. The three shaded areas are single phase. All other areas are two phase

If a binary eutectic diagram is hatched, as shown in Figure 2.7, the only phases that exist are those in one of the three shaded regions. A combination of temperature and overall composition that specifies a position in a clear region of the diagram such as (B, T) in Figure 2.7 indicates that the alloy consists of two phases. The composition of each of the two phases is given by the intersection of the constant temperature or isothermal line with the phase boundaries at C_α and C_β in Figure 2.7. An alloy of any overall composition between C_α and C_β at temperature T will be composed of α phase of composition C_α and β phase of composition C_β. The composition of a phase is simply the proportion of each of the two constituent elements that are present in that phase. Thus the composition C_α is 10% B, 90% A while the composition C_β is 80% B, 20% A, whereas the proportion of the phase is the amount of that phase which is present within the total alloy. The confusing aspect is that often both proportion and composition are expressed as percentages. The proportions of the two phases are given by the so called Lever Rule. Its name derives from the analogy with the balancing of a beam in statics and it states that if the composition of the two phases is C_α and C_β and the overall composition of the alloy is C then the proportions of the two phases present are given by the formulae below:

$$\text{Proportion of phase } \alpha = \frac{C_\beta - C}{C_\beta - C_\alpha} \times 100\%$$

$$\text{Proportion of phase } \beta = \frac{C - C_\alpha}{C_\beta - C_\alpha} \times 100\%$$

So the proportions 'balance' about the composition C in the same way that masses would balance about a fulcrum at C in statics.

2.8 Coring in a binary alloy

When binary alloys solidify they frequently do so with a non-homogeneous distribution of the alloying elements throughout the grains. This is because the first solid that forms is of different composition from the liquid from which it forms. In the case of a primary solid solution of a binary eutectic alloy the composition of the first solid that forms is lower in the addition element, than is the liquid from which it forms or the average composition of the alloy. Because diffusion takes place relatively quickly in the liquid but extremely slowly in the solid, and because the separation of relatively pure solid concentrates the solute in the remaining liquid, the successive layers of solid that solidify are progressively richer in the addition element than was the first solid to form. Metallographically one frequently finds a dendritic structure to the grains in which the core of the dendrites has a quite different composition from the material between the dendrite arms, which is the last material to solidify. It is possible to calculate the variation of composition in the final cast product of a primary solid solution of a binary eutectic alloy. The assumptions made are that equilibrium conditions apply to the compositions on either side of the advancing solid liquid interface, that complete diffusion occurs in the liquid, that no diffusion at all occurs in the solid and that the mean solid composition is the mean of that most recently formed and the first solid to form. These assumptions are usually reasonable. The solidification process can perhaps best be followed by reference to Figure 2.8. Liquid of

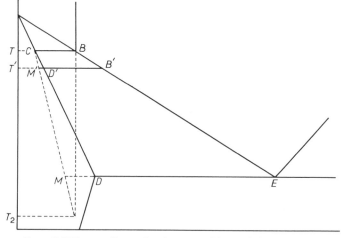

Figure 2.8 Diagram illustrating the composition variations in coring

composition B starts to solidify at temperature T producing solid whose composition is C. As the temperature falls to T', solid of composition D' separates from liquid whose composition is B'. The mean composition of the solid is clearly between C and D' and is shown as M'. As the temperature falls, this progression continues until the mean solid composition becomes equal to B, whereupon all the alloy must be solid. If, however, the eutectic temperature is reached, as shown in Figure 2.8, before this occurs, the final mean solid composition is M and some eutectic solid of composition E solidifies between the dendrites.

2.9 Quantitative metallography

The ability to measure the characteristics of a micro-structure is particularly important if quantitative relationships are to be developed between the micro-structure and the properties of the material. Thus, the relationship between grain size and yield strength is a fundamental one, as is the relationship between fatigue

strength and inclusion content. The two basic types of micro-
structure are a grain structure and a structure of particles in a
matrix. The measurements on which the calculations are based are
of the intercepts of the elements of the micro-structure with a line or
grid of lines ruled over a random section through the micro-
structure as shown in Figure 2.9. Thus, for a grain structure it is

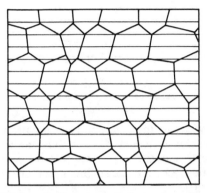

Figure 2.9 Schematic diagram of a grain structure with a roster
of measuring lines

simple to calculate the mean linear intercept M, the ASTM grain
size S, the 95% confidence limit C as a percentage of M and the
grain boundary area per unit volume U from the formulae given
below:

$$M = L/N$$

$$S = 1 + 2 \times \frac{\ln\left(\frac{0.226}{M}\right)}{\ln 2}$$

$$C = 70/\sqrt{N}$$

$$U = 2/M$$

where L = length of line and N = number of intercepts.

These formulae are valid for a random line through a structure
that is non-directional. If the grain structure is elongated then a
number of random lines must be taken through the structure to
obtain a statistically valid answer.

If the micro-structure consists of particles in a matrix the analysis
is a little more complex. The calculation is based on the analysis of a
scanning television type image, which has a known number of
picture points across the frame and a known number of lines con-
stituting the measuring frame. This is illustrated in Figure 2.10.

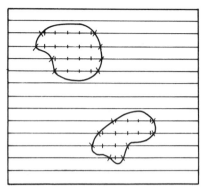

Figure 2.10 Schematic diagram of particles in a matrix with a roster of measuring lines

Knowing the width of the frame in both picture points W_1 and in millimetres on the specimen W_2 and the number of lines in the scanned frame H, a number of features of the particle distribution can be calculated. The measurements taken are those of the total area of the particles in picture points A, the number of intercepts of the scanned line with a particle I and the total number of separate particles in the frame P. The following formulae are used:

$$\text{Volume fraction} = \frac{A}{H \times W_1}$$

$$\text{Mean particle size} = \frac{2A}{I} \times \frac{W_2}{W_1}$$

$$\text{Surface-to-volume ratio} = 2 \times \frac{I}{A} \times \frac{W_1}{W_2}$$

A, I and P are available from the analysis of a scanned television image or they can be found by laborious measurements from a grid superimposed on the projected image. A shape factor can be introduced to assess whether the particles are approximately spherical in shape and uniform in size. If we define the shape factor F as

$$F = \frac{I^2}{A \times P}$$

a series of uniform randomly sectioned spheres will give a value of $\frac{3}{8}\pi$ or 1.178. If the particles are spherical but non-uniform in size or if their width is much greater than their height, then the value of F will be significantly below this value. If the value is significantly above 1.178 the particles are either re-entrant or tall and thin. If the particles are found to be spherical then the other statistics available are

$$\text{Particles/unit volume} = \frac{\pi P^2}{4I W_1 H} \times \left(\frac{W_1}{W_2}\right)^3$$

$$\text{Mean volume of particle} = \frac{4IA}{\pi P^2} \times \left(\frac{W_2}{W_1}\right)^3$$

$$\text{Mean surface area per particle} = \frac{8}{\pi}\left(\frac{2IW_2}{PW_1}\right)^2$$

PROGRAMS

Program 2.1: Atoms on a crystal plane

As discussed in Section 2.2, the graphical representation of the positions of atoms on a crystal plane has applications in deformation of crystals and in interpretation of diffraction patterns. As it stands the program does not index each atom plotted but it could easily be extended to do that, making it more versatile.

```
100 REM 2.1 ATOMS ON CRYSTAL PLANES
110 INIT
120 PAGE
130 REM CHOOSE CUBIC TYPE
140 PRINT "ENTER 1 FOR SIMPLE C, 2 FOR B C C, 3 FOR F C C ";
150 INPUT I
160 IF I=1 THEN 250
170 IF I=2 THEN 220
180 IF I<>3 THEN 140
190 P=4
200 D=5
210 GO TO 270
220 P=2
230 D=5
240 GO TO 270
250 P=1
260 D=5
270 REM SET UP ATOM POSITIONS
280 DIM A(P*D^2),B(P*D^2),C(P*D^2),R(P*D^2),T(P*D^2)
290 REM SELECT A PLANE
300 PRINT "ENTER MILLER INDECES OF A PLANE H,K,L ";
310 INPUT H,K,L
320 J=1
330 A=0
340 B=0
350 C=0
360 FOR U=1 TO D
370 FOR V=1 TO D
380 FOR W=1 TO D
390 REM CUBE CORNERS
400 X=U-1
410 Y=V-1
420 Z=W-1
430 GOSUB 820
440 NEXT W
450 NEXT V
460 NEXT U
470 IF P=1 THEN 900
480 IF P=4 THEN 610
490 REM BODY CENTRES
500 FOR U=1 TO D
```

```
510 FOR V=1 TO D
520 FOR W=1 TO D
530 X=U-1+0.5
540 Y=V-1+0.5
550 Z=W-1+0.5
560 GOSUB 820
570 NEXT W
580 NEXT V
590 NEXT U
600 GO TO 900
610 REM FACE CENTRES
620 FOR U=1 TO D
630 FOR V=1 TO D
640 FOR W=1 TO D
650 X=U-1+0.5
660 Y=V-1+0.5
670 Z=W-1
680 GOSUB 820
690 X=U-1
700 Y=V-1+0.5
710 Z=W-1+0.5
720 GOSUB 820
730 X=U-1+0.5
740 Y=V-1
750 Z=W-1+0.5
760 GOSUB 820
770 NEXT W
780 NEXT V
790 NEXT U
810 GO TO 900
820 REM CHECK INTERCEPTION
830 IF X*H+Y*L-Z*K<>0 THEN 890
840 A(J)=X
850 B(J)=Y
860 C(J)=Z
870 R(J)=(A(J)^2+B(J)^2+C(J)^2)^0.5
880 J=J+1
890 RETURN
900 REM PLOT POSITIONS
910 T=0
920 MOVE 20,20
930 PRINT "+"
940 FOR I=2 TO J-1
950 T(I)=(A(I)*A(2)+B(I)*B(2)+C(I)*C(2))/R(I)/R(2)-1.0E-8
955 T(I)=ACS(T(I))
960 MOVE 20+10*R(I)*COS(T(I)),20+10*R(I)*SIN(T(I))
970 PRINT "+";
980 NEXT I
990 MOVE 0,8
1000 PRINT "PRESS RETURN FOR ANOTHER PLANE "
1010 INPUT A$
1020 IF A$="" THEN 100
1030 END
```

Program notes

This program allows the operator to choose simple cubic, body-centred-cubic, or face-centred-cubic crystal lattices and to plot the distribution of atoms on any nominated plane in any one of those three crystal structures. It works by calculating the coordinates of each atom in a three-dimensional array of 125 unit cells and then inspecting each set of coordinates to see whether it is intersected by the specified plane.

(1) If the coordinates are x, y and z and the plane is (h,k,l) the criterion for intersection is that

$$hx + ky + lz = 0$$

(2) Lines 100–260 allow the choice of crystal structure and select values for P, the number of atoms per unit cell and D the number of unit cells along the axis of the array.

(3) After the required plane has been entered at line 310, lines 390–460 set up the coordinates of the corners of the unit cubes for the array of atoms chosen.

(4) Lines 490–590 add the body-centred atoms if those are required and lines 610–790 add the face-centred atoms if they are required.

(5) After each set of three coordinates has been assigned the sub-routine 830–890 inspects for an intersection. If it is found, the coordinates are added to the arrays A(I), B(I) and C(I). If not a new set of coordinates is assigned and they are tested for intersection.

(6) For convenience, intersection with the plane $(h,k,\bar{l})$ is tested as this intersects the positive quadrant of the atomic array, whereas (h,k,l) does not if all the indices are positive. The maximum number of intersections is the number of atoms per unit cell multiplied by the maximum number of unit cells intersected. Thus the arrays A, B and C are dimensioned to a size of P × D. The reader can easily verify this in the case of simple cubic and body-centred-cubic but the face-centred-cubic case is a little more complex and needs a maximum of only 60 sets of coordinates, not the 100 allowed for by this simple formula.

(7) Having selected the coordinates A(I), B(I) and C(I) for each of the atoms intersected by the plane, lines 900–980 plot the position of those atoms on the plane of the VDU screen. To do this point 1 is taken as the origin of the plot and is plotted in line 920 at screen coordinates 20,20. The planar coordinates of the atom positions are plotted as polar coordinates using the angle T(I) and the radius R(I) which is the distance of the atom from the origin of the plot and has already been calculated at line 870. Because of the way T(I) is defined the angle T(2) is always zero so this point is always plotted along the horizontal axis (see Figure 2.11).

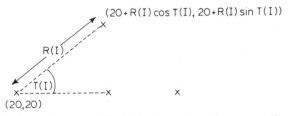

Figure 2.11 Polar coordinates used in plotting the position of atoms on a plane

(8) The program as written uses a total of 125 unit cells and in this form it runs quite quickly. If a more complete plot is required then a larger number of unit cells must be used and this is done by altering the value of D to 6 or 7.

The graphical display in lines 900 to 990 will need to be modified for other computers. Line 950 will still be used but the coordinates on the screen at lines 920, 960 and 990 will need to be changed.

Program 2.2: Dislocations

Three programs are introduced here which are assembled together for simplicity of selection. They all use graphical representation and cover the strains around a dislocation, the force between like dislocations and the width of a dissociated dislocation.

The coordinates used in the graphical representation are, of course, only valid for the Tektronix computer but a slight modification will enable the programs to be adapted for any other graphics system.

```
100 REM 2.2 DISLOCATIONS
110 PAGE
120 PRINT "STRAIN,FORCE OR WIDTH ? (S,F or W) ";
130 INPUT A$
140 IF A$="F" THEN 600
150 IF A$="W" THEN 1000
160 IF A$<>"S" THEN 120
200 REM STRAIN AROUND DISLOCATIONS
210 PAGE
220 PRINT "STRAIN AROUND A DISLOCATION "
230 PRINT "EDGE OR SCREW (E OR S) ";
240 INPUT A$
250 PRINT "HOW MANY UNIT LATTICE VECTORS AWAY? ";
260 INPUT A
270 IF A<1 THEN 250
280 SET DEGREES
290 IF A$="S" THEN 430
300 IF A$<>"E" THEN 230
310 MOVE 65,50
320 FOR I=10 TO 360 STEP 10
330 X=65+20/A*COS(I)*SIN(I)
340 Y=50+20/A*SIN(I)^2
350 IF I<180 THEN 370
360 Y=100-Y
370 DRAW X,Y
380 NEXT I
390 MOVE 65+12/A,50+5/A
400 PRINT "COMPRESSION"
410 MOVE 65+12/A,50-5/A
420 PRINT "EXPANSION"
430 MOVE 65+40/A,50
440 FOR I=10 TO 360 STEP 10
450 X=65+40/A*COS(I)
460 Y=50+40/A*SIN(I)
470 DRAW X,Y
480 NEXT I
490 PRINT "  SHEAR"
500 MOVE 0,5
```

```
510 GO TO 120
600 REM FORCE BETWEEN DISLOCATIONS
610 PAGE
620 PRINT "EDGE OR SCREW? (E OR S) ";
630 INPUT A$
640 IF A$="E" OR A$="S" THEN 660
650 GO TO 620
660 PRINT "ENTER COORDINATES OF SECOND DISLOCATION
665 PRINT "(FROM -50 TO +50)";
670 INPUT X,Y
680 IF A$="E" THEN 790
690 R=X^2+Y^2
700 U=33.3*X/R
710 V=33.3*Y/R
720 X=X+65
730 Y=Y+50
740 MOVE 65,50
750 PRINT "."
760 MOVE X,Y
770 RDRAW U,V
780 GO TO 120
790 U=50*X*(X^2-Y^2)/(X^2+Y^2)^2
800 V=50*Y*(3*X^2+Y^2)/(X^2+Y^2)^2
810 X=X+65
820 Y=Y+50
830 MOVE 65,50
840 PRINT "1H_"
850 MOVE X,Y
860 RDRAW U,0
870 MOVE X,Y
880 RDRAW 0,V
890 MOVE X,Y
900 MOVE 0,5
910 GO TO 120
1000 REM WIDTH OF DISLOCATION
1010 PAGE
1020 PRINT "ENTER STACKING FAULT ENERGY JOULES/M^2 ";
1030 INPUT G
1040 D=0.5/G
1050 MOVE 65-D/2,10
1060 RDRAW 0,80
1070 MOVE 65+D/2,10
1080 RDRAW 0,80
1090 PRINT "SPACING =";0.163/G;"nm FOR ALUMINIUM"
1100 MOVE 0,5
1110 GO TO 120
1120 END
```

Program notes

(1) Lines 100–160 allow the selection of program segment. If the strain program is selected, the type of dislocation must be specified at line 240 and the distance from the dislocation core at line 260. If an edge dislocation is selected, lines 320–380 draw the compressive and dilatational strain which surrounds the dislocation, these being then labelled at lines 400 and 420.

(2) The shear strain surrounding either an edge or screw dislocation is drawn at lines 440–480 and labelled at 490. In use, this program very clearly illustrates to the student the rapid variation of strain as the core of the dislocation is approached.

(3) The second part of the program illustrates the force between a

pair of edge dislocations or a pair of screw dislocations. The coordinates of the second dislocation are entered at line 670 and if the dislocations are of screw type the force between them is plotted in lines 690–770 as a vector whose length is proportional to the force and whose direction is the direction of the force.

(4) Edge dislocations have a more complex force field and in this case lines 790–880 plot a pair of vectors, one parallel to the slip plane, which is chosen to be horizontal, and one perpendicular to the slip plane. Use of the program will show that if the second dislocation lies at 45° with respect to the slip plane then there is no force on it parallel to the slip plane and so it will not move on the slip plane. Again the magnitude of the forces is critically dependent on the separation of the two dislocations.

(5) The final very short program section enables the reader to visualize the effects of stacking fault energy on the width of a dissociated dislocation.

The only value of this very brief program is its ability to assist in visualizing the influence of stacking fault energy and in assuring that the units of the separation between the two partials are correct. The calculation of separation is done for aluminium but changing the constant in line 1090 enables the calculation to be done for any other material.

Program 2.3: Stereographic projection

Since writing a computer program that will cover all the aspects of the crystallographic use of the stereographic projection would be rather a protracted exercise, the program that follows deals with the standard 001 projection for a cubic crystal and allows any other crystal pole to be plotted on that projection. Because it is essentially a graphical display, the detailed graphic commands of the program will be different for different types of computer. The version listed operates on the Tektronics 4050 series, where the graphics are versatile and of high quality. It is necessary to use a computer where high resolution graphics and alpha numeric characters may be mixed, otherwise the display cannot be annotated properly.

```
70 REM 2.3 STEREOGRAPHIC PROJECTION
80 PAGE
90 PRINT "STEREOGRAPHIC PROJECTION PLOTS"
100 REM FILL ARRAYS WITH DATA
110 REM REPRESENTING A CIRCLE
120 INIT
130 DIM X(72),Y(72)
140 SET DEGREES
150 FOR I=1 TO 72
160 X(I)=50*COS(I*5)
170 Y(I)=50*SIN(I*5)
180 NEXT I
```

```
190 REM
200 PAGE
210 REM DEFINE WINDOW AND VIEWPORT
220 WINDOW -50,50,-50,50
230 VIEWPORT 30,124,3,97
240 GOSUB 920
250 WINDOW 0,71,-35,35
260 GOSUB 920
270 WINDOW -71,0,-35,35
280 GOSUB 920
290 WINDOW -35,35,-71,0
300 GOSUB 920
310 WINDOW -35,35,0,71
320 GOSUB 920
330 WINDOW 30,130,0,100
340 MOVE 30,50
350 DRAW 130,50
360 MOVE 80,0
370 DRAW 80,100
380 MOVE 45,14
390 DRAW 116,86
400 MOVE 115,15
410 DRAW 45,85
420 VIEWPORT 30,130,0,100
430 MOVE 76,0
440 PRINT "100";
450 MOVE 125,49
460 PRINT "010";
470 MOVE 81,50
480 PRINT "001";
490 HOME
500 J=0
510 MOVE 0,100-2*J
520 PRINT "ENTER H,K,L"
530 INPUT H,K,L
540 IF H<>0 THEN 560
550 H=1.0E-6
560 IF K<>0 THEN 580
570 K=1.0E-6
580 IF L<>0 THEN 600
590 L=1.0E-6
600 SET DEGREES
610 T=ATN(K/H)
620 IF H>0 THEN 670
630 IF K>0 THEN 660
640 T=T+180
650 GO TO 670
660 T=T+180
670 G=ACS(L/(L*L+H*H+K*K)^0.5)
680 R=50*TAN(G/2)
690 X=80+R*SIN(T)
700 Y=50-R*COS(T)
710 VIEWPORT 30,124,3,97
720 MOVE X,Y
730 SCALE 1,1
740 RMOVE -0.5*1.55,-0.5*1.88
750 PRINT "+";
760 RMOVE 0.5*1.55,0.5*1.88
770 WINDOW 30,130,0,100
780 MOVE X,Y
790 IF H<>1.0E-6 THEN 810
800 H=0
810 IF K<>1.0E-6 THEN 830
820 K=0
830 IF L<>1.0E-6 THEN 850
840 L=0
850 PRINT H;K;L
```

```
860 HOME
870 J=J+3
880 IF J>50 THEN 120
890 GO TO 510
900 REM
910 REM
920 REM SUBROUTINE TO DRAW CIRCLE
930 MOVE X(72),Y(72)
940 DRAW X,Y
950 RETURN
```

Program notes

(1) Lines 100–200 set up a series of XY coordinates which describe a circle and are later used in the sub-routine at line 920.

(2) Lines 210–320 draw the outer circle and the traces of the (011), $(0\bar{1}1)$, (101) and $(\bar{1}01)$ planes and lines 330–410 draw the traces of the (110), $(1\bar{1}0)$, (100) and (010) planes.

(3) At line 520 indices of the required pole are entered. In order to prevent the illegal operation of dividing by zero, if H or K or L are zero they are allocated a value of 10^{-6} in lines 540–590.

(4) T is the angle that the plotted position of pole HKL makes with the 100 pole of the stereographic projection, and that is calculated at line 610.

(5) In order to get the absolute value of the angle T correct, since it is only determined by the value of its tangent, line 620 checks whether H is positive and if not adds 180° to the value of T.

(6) G is the angle which the pole HKL makes with the 001 pole and that is calculated in line 670. Knowledge of G allows the length R to be calculated which is the distance of the plotted point HKL from the centre of the stereographic projection.

(7) X and Y coordinates of the point HKL are calculated in lines 690 and 700 from the R and T values already calculated above, and these are then plotted in lines 710–770.

(8) At line 780 the indices H, K and L are plotted.

Prior to plotting, a value of zero must be reinstated for 10^{-6} where that value has been assigned earlier in the program.

(9) At line 890 the program returns for the input of another value of H, K and L.

The particular points to note in this program are first, that it is necessary to replace zero with a very small number as an error occurs if this is denominator of a fraction. Secondly, that the values of angles need to be specified within the angular range from 0° to 360° not simply −90° to 90° if calculated from their tangent or sine or 0° to 180° if calculated from their cosine. This can be done by inspecting the sign of the numerator and denominator of the fractions from which the value of the angle is calculated.

Program 2.4: Atomic and weight percent compositions

```
100 REM 2.4 ATOMIC AND WEIGHT PERCENT COMPOSITIONS
110 PAGE
120 PRINT "1. Atomic % from Weight %"
130 PRINT "2. weight % from Atomic %"
140 PRINT "Enter 1 or 2 ";
150 INPUT X
160 PRINT
200 PRINT "How many elements? ";
210 INPUT N
220 PRINT
230 IF N<11 THEN 260
240 PRINT "Maximum number is 10"
250 GO TO 200
260 IF X=2 THEN 470
270 IF X<>1 THEN 460
280 REM ATOMIC %
290 DIM A(N),M(N),W(N)
300 S=0
310 T=0
320 FOR I=1 TO N
330 PRINT "ENTER  Weight %(";I;"), Atomic weight (";I;") ";
340 INPUT W(I),M(I)
350 S=S+W(I)/M(I)
360 T=T+W(I)
370 NEXT I
380 PRINT
390 IF T=100 THEN 420
400 PRINT "Sum of weight % must be 100"
410 GO TO 300
420 FOR I=1 TO N
430 PRINT "Atomic % (";I;")=";W(I)/M(I)/S*100
440 NEXT I
450 PRINT
460 GO TO 120
470 REM WEIGHT %
480 DIM A(N),M(N),W(N)
490 S=0
500 T=0
510 FOR I=1 TO N
520 PRINT "ENTER  Atomic %(";I;"), Atomic weight (";I;") ";
530 INPUT A(I),M(I)
540 S=S+A(I)*M(I)
550 T=T+A(I)
560 NEXT I
570 PRINT
580 IF T=100 THEN 610
590 PRINT "Sum of ATOMIC % must be 100"
600 GO TO 490
610 FOR I=1 TO N
620 PRINT "Weight % (";I;")=";A(I)*M(I)/S*100
630 NEXT I
640 PRINT
650 GO TO 120
660 END
670 END
```

Program notes

(1) Having chosen which way the conversion is to be done, the
number of elements are entered, followed by the weight percents

and atomic weights or the atomic percents and the atomic weights. The calculation is then done and the results are printed.

(2) Lines 120 to 250 allow the direction of the conversion to be indicated and the number of elements to be entered. A suggested maximum number of elements of ten is included in the program but this is in no way a necessary limitation of the capability of the program.

(3) Lines 280 to 460 allow the conversion from weight percent to atomic percent. For each element in turn, lines 300 to 410 calculate the variable S which is the sum of the quotients of the weight percents divided by the atomic weights and the variable T which is the sum of the weight percents. At line 390 if the weight percents do not add to 100 this is pointed out and new data are requested.

(4) Finally, in line 430 the atomic percent is calculated for each element in turn and the values printed.

An exactly similar sequence is followed in lines 470 to 650, but this time to calculate the weight percent from the atomic percent. The structure of the program is identical but the variable, S, is now the sum of the products of the atomic percents and atomic weights. The line 620 where the weight percent is calculated is of a slightly different form from line 430.

Program 2.5: Hume–Rothery primary solid solubility

```
100 REM 2.5 HUME-ROTHERY PRIMARY SOLID SOLUBILITY
110 PAGE
120 PRINT "This is a simple application of the Hume-Rothery"
130 PRINT "rules for primary solubility. The size factor"
140 PRINT "rule is normally obeyed but the others are not"
145 PRINT "always good predictors."
150 PRINT
160 PRINT "List all the available metals? (Y or N) ";
170 INPUT A$
180 IF A$<>"Y" THEN 250
190 PAGE
200 READ A$,A,B,C
210 IF A$="Z" THEN 240
220 PRINT A$
230 GO TO 200
240 RESTORE
250 DATA "NA",1.855,0.9,1
260 DATA "ZN",1.33,1.5,2
270 DATA "CD",1.486,1.4,2
280 DATA "GA",1.33,1.6,3
290 DATA "BI",1.56,1.8,5
300 DATA "AG",1.44,1.7,1
310 DATA "SB",1.45,1.9,5
320 DATA "AS",1.25,2,5
330 DATA "HG",1.5,1.9,2
340 DATA "SN",1.508,1.8,4
350 DATA "MG",1.6,1.2,2
360 DATA "LI",1.515,1,1
370 DATA "BA",2.17,0.9,1
380 DATA "IN",1.45,1.5,3
390 DATA "TL",1.7,1.4,3
400 DATA "PB",1.745,1.8,4
410 DATA "AL",1.43,1.5,3
```

```
420 DATA "CA",1.975,1,2
430 DATA "BE",1.125,1.4,2
440 DATA "CU",1.275,1.7,1
450 DATA "AU",1.435,2.1,1
460 DATA "K",2.25,0.8,1
470 DATA "RB",2.49,0.8,1
480 DATA "SR",2.13,1,2
490 DATA "CS",2.63,0.7,1
500 DATA "Z",0,0,0
510 REM****************APPLY RULES
520 GO TO 550
530 PRINT "ELEMENT NOT FOUND "
540 RESTORE
550 PRINT "SOLID SOLUBILITY"
560 PRINT
570 B=0
580 PRINT "ENTER FIRST ELEMENT ";
590 INPUT A$
600 READ Z$,A1,P1,V1
610 IF A$=Z$ THEN 640
620 IF Z$="Z" THEN 530
630 GO TO 600
640 PRINT "ENTER SECOND ELEMENT ";
650 INPUT B$
660 RESTORE
670 READ Y$,A2,P2,V2
680 IF B$=Y$ THEN 710
690 IF Y$="Z" THEN 530
700 GO TO 670
710 R=A1/A2
720 IF R<1.15 AND R>0.85 THEN 760
730 PRINT "Size factor unfavourable for primary solubility"
740 B=1
750 PRINT
760 Q=P1-P2
770 IF Q^2<0.1 THEN 800
780 PRINT "Solubility may be restricted due to ";
785 PRINT "compound formation"
790 PRINT
800 IF V1>V2 THEN 880
810 IF V2>V1 THEN 850
820 PRINT "EQUALLY SOLUBLE IN EACH OTHER"
830 PRINT
840 GO TO 900
850 PRINT B$;" more soluble in ";A$;" than ";A$;" in ";B$
860 PRINT
870 GO TO 900
880 PRINT A$;" more soluble in ";B$;" than ";B$;" in ";A$
890 PRINT
900 IF Z$<>"CU" AND Z$<>"AG" AND Z$<>"AU" THEN 950
910 IF V2=1 OR B=1 THEN 1000
920 X1=(1.4-V1)/(V2-V1)*100
930 PRINT "Solubility of ";B$;" in ";A$;" =";X1;"Atomic %"
940 GO TO 1000
950 IF Y$<>"CU" AND Y$<>"AG" AND Y$<>"AU" THEN 1000
960 IF B=1 THEN 1000
970 X2=(1.4-V2)/(V1-V2)*100
980 PRINT
990 PRINT "Solubility of ";A$;" in ";B$;" =";X2;"Atomic %"
1000 PRINT
1010 RESTORE
1020 GO TO 550
1030 END
```

Program notes

(1) The three Hume–Rothery rules for primary solid solubility are

applied by the program to data on each of the two elements forming the alloy and an indication is given of the likely extent of primary solubility.

(2) A disclaimer is printed at lines 120–140 indicating that although the rule stating that extensive solubility will not occur if the size difference between atoms is greater than 14% is normally obeyed, the other 'rules' are not such good predictors. It is then possible to list the 25 elements whose data are stored in the program. They are the most common non-transition metal elements.

(3) The data occupying lines 250 to 490 and line 500 is required to terminate the searches.

(4) The chemical symbol for the first element is entered at line 580 and the DATA statements are searched for that symbol. If it is not found, the fact is recorded at line 530, the data count is restored at line 540 and the program restarted.

(5) The second element is similarly entered and searched at line 640–700.

(6) Lines 710–730 calculate the size difference between the two atoms and if this is too large, indicate that primary solubility is unfavourable due to the difference in size. The variable B is assigned a value of 1 so that extensive solubility is not calculated later.

(7) Lines 760 and 770 compare the electro-negativities of the two elements and if the difference between these is too great, indicate that solubility may be restricted due to compound formation.

(8) Lines 800–880 test which element has the greater number of valency electrons and as a result indicate which element is likely to be more soluble in the other.

(9) Line 900 checks whether the first element is Cu, Ag or Au, if so it calculates the likely solubility of the second element in the first, unless $B = 1$ indicating that the size factor is unfavourable.

(10) Line 950 checks whether the second element is Cu, Ag or Au, in which case it calculates the solubility of the first element in the second.

Clearly, such a program is a fairly trite exercise in alloy theory. However, as the program contains all the data on the possible elements, a very rapid assessment can be made of the likely primary solubilities of any pair of elements chosen. 25 elements allows a total of 600 alloys to be covered.

Program 2.6: Binary eutectic equilibrium diagram

As written, this program contains the data for the equilibrium diagram shown in Figure 2.12. It is easy to alter these data or indeed to modify the program so that the fixed temperatures and composi-

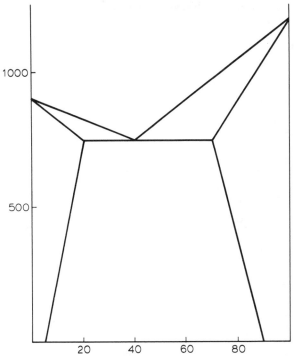

Figure 2.12 Binary eutectic equilibrium diagram used in Program 2.6

tions can be specified. However, it is simpler to see how the
program works with a standard set of fixed points. The program
calls for the temperature and overall composition of the alloy, it
then calculates the compositions of the phase boundary intersections for the particular temperature input, and on the basis of
these data, decides in which phase field the input composition and
temperature combination lies. It then calculates the proportion of
each of the phases that are present and their compositions and prints
as output the names of the phases, the proportions of the phases and
their compositions.

```
100 REM 2.6 BINARY EUTECTIC DIAGRAM
110 PAGE
120 DIM K(6),T(7),C(7)
130 FOR I=1 TO 7
140 READ T(I),C(I)
150 NEXT I
160 DATA 900,0,0,5,750,20,750,40,750,70,0,90,1200,100
170 PRINT "ENTER TEMPERATURE,COMPOSITION ";
180 INPUT S,B
190 IF B>0 OR B<100 THEN 220
200 PRINT "RANGE OF B IS 0 TO 100"
210 GO TO 180
```

```
220 REM CALCULATE COMPOSITIONS K(H) FROM PHASE BOUNDARIES
230 H=1
240 I=1
250 J=3
260 GOSUB 920
270 J=4
280 GOSUB 920
290 I=7
300 GOSUB 920
310 J=5
320 GOSUB 920
330 I=2
340 J=3
350 GOSUB 920
360 I=6
370 J=5
380 GOSUB 920
390 REM DECIDE ON PHASE FIELD
400 IF B<=C(3) OR B=>C(5) THEN 420
410 IF S=T(4) THEN 950
420 IF S<T(4) THEN 650
430 IF B>K(1) AND B<K(2) THEN 860
440 IF B>K(3) AND B<K(4) THEN 810
450 IF B<=K(1) THEN 580
460 IF B=>K(4) THEN 550
470 IF B=>K(2) AND B<=K(3) THEN 500
480 PRINT "ERROR IN DATA"
490 GO TO 170
500 A$="liquid"
510 B$=""
520 I=2
530 J=3
540 GO TO 600
550 A$="beta"
560 B$=""
570 GO TO 600
580 A$="alpha"
590 B$=""
600 PRINT A$
610 PRINT "single phase"
620 PRINT B;"percent of element A"
630 PRINT
640 GO TO 170
650 IF B<=K(5) THEN 580
660 IF B=>K(6) THEN 550
670 A$="alpha"
680 B$="    plus       beta"
690 I=5
700 J=6
710 REM CALCULATE COMPOSITIONS
720 X=K(I)
730 Y=K(J)
740 P=(K(J)-B)/(K(J)-K(I))
750 Q=(B-K(I))/(K(J)-K(I))
760 PRINT A$;B$
770 PRINT P,Q;"  proportion of phases"
780 PRINT X,Y;"  percent of element A"
790 PRINT
800 GO TO 170
810 A$="beta"
820 B$="    plus       liquid"
830 I=3
840 J=4
850 GO TO 710
860 A$="alpha"
870 B$="    plus     liquid"
880 I=1
```

```
890 J=2
900 GO TO 710
910 END
920 K(H)=C(I)+(S-T(I))*(C(J)-C(I))/(T(J)-T(I))
930 H=H+1
940 RETURN
950 REM EUTECTIC TEMP
960 PRINT "EUTECTIC TEMP 3 PHASES IN EQUM"
970 PRINT
980 GO TO 170
990 END
```

Program notes

(1) Three arrays are used in the program, T(7) for the temperatures of the fixed points, C(7) for the compositions of the fixed points and K(6) for the points at which the phase boundaries intersect the input temperature.

(2) Lines 120 to 160 simply fill the arrays T and C with the data for the fixed points.

(3) Lines 170 to 210 input and correct the data of temperature and composition.

(4) Lines 220 to 380 calculate the compositions at which the input temperature S intersects the phase boundaries.

(5) The sub-routine which calculates the formula for each phase boundary is given in lines 920–940.

(6) Having calculated the compositions K, lines 390–490 indicate in which phase field the input temperature and composition lie.

(7) Lines 500–700 allocate names to phases and give the integer variables I and J values specific to the phase field. If the phase field is single phase then there is no calculation of composition or proportion necessary as the proportion of the phase is 100% and its composition is as input at the beginning of the program.

(8) For a two-phase field, however, a calculation of composition and proportion must be made and this is done in lines 720–800.

(9) The final section of the program lines 950–980 are used if the three eutectic phases are in equilibrium with each other, which of course occurs only if the input temperature is the eutectic temperature and if the composition range is within the eutectic isothermal.

Use of this program enables the student to become familiar with the effect that changing temperature at a given composition or changing composition at a given temperature has on the composition and proportion of the phases that are present within an alloy. As an illustration choose a temperature of 800°C and vary the composition from 10% up to 80% when five different phase fields will be traversed. Or, alternatively, choose a composition of 10% and vary the temperature from 100°C to 1000°C whereupon a series of four different phase fields will be traversed.

Program 2.7: Coring

As discussed in Section 2.8, this program calculates the variation in composition within the primary solid phase during non-equilibrium solidification of an alloy from a eutectic system. It also indicates whether any eutectic solid is likely to form from the final liquid to solidify.

Having entered the melting point of the pure metal, the eutectic temperature, the maximum solid solubility and the eutectic composition, the program then calculates the temperature T_2 at which the mean solid composition will equal the input composition. This must be the temperature at which the whole alloy is solid. The temperature at which the first solid forms T_1 is calculated from the liquidus line and successive solidification steps are calculated for drops of temperature of $(T_1 - T_2)/20$ and the computer prints the solid composition most recently formed, the average solid composition, the proportion of the alloy that is solid and the composition of the liquid. If the temperature T_2 is below the eutectic temperature Y, solidification terminates at temperature Y and the print-out indicates this. Thus, for instance, a typical case would show an input composition of liquid of 9% of solute resulting in solid whose composition varies from 2.7%–12.2%, liquid whose composition varies from 9% up to 40.5% and an average solid composition which varies from 2.7%–7.4%. In this particular case some 5% of the material solidified as eutectic solid at the end of the solidification process.

```
100 REM 2.7 CORING
110 PAGE
120 PRINT "ENTER MELTING POINT, EUTECTIC TEMP ";
130 INPUT X,Y
140 PRINT "ENTER MAX SOLID SOLN, EUTECTIC COMPN ";
150 INPUT U,V
160 PRINT "ENTER COMPOSITION OF LIQUID %A ";
170 INPUT A
180 IF A>100 OR A<0 THEN 160
190 GOSUB 410
200 PRINT "FIRST SOLID ";C1;"%"
210 PRINT "SOLID%        AV. SOLID %        PROP OF SOLID";
215 PRINT "    LIQUID%"
220 FOR I=1 TO 20
230 T=T1-(I-0.5)*(T1-T2)/20
240 GOSUB 460
250 PRINT N,D,P,C2
260 IF T<=Y THEN 290
270 NEXT I
280 GO TO 360
290 PRINT
300 PRINT "RANGE OF SOLID ";C1;" TO ";N;"%A"
310 PRINT
320 PRINT "PROP OF SOLID ";P
330 PRINT
340 PRINT "EUTECTIC SOLID ";V;"%"
350 GO TO 400
360 PRINT
370 PRINT "LAST LIQUID ";C2;"%"
380 PRINT
```

```
390 PRINT "RANGE OF SOLID ";C1;" TO ";N;" %A"
400 END
410 REM SOL & LIQ TEMP
420 T1=X-(X-Y)/V*A
430 C1=A*U/V
440 T2=T1-2*(T1-Y)*(A-C1)/(U-C1)
450 RETURN
460 REM COMP  SOL & LIQ
470 N=(X-T)/(X-Y)*U
480 D=C1+(T1-T)/(T1-Y)*(U-C1)/2
490 C2=(X-T)/(X-Y)*V
500 P=(C2-A)/(C2-D)
510 RETURN
```

Program notes

(1) Lines 120–170 allow the melting point, eutectic temperature, maximum solid solubility, eutectic composition and initial composition of liquid to be entered.

(2) The liquidus temperature T1, first solid composition C1 and final solidification temperature T2 are calculated in the sub-routine at lines 410 and the progressive solid and liquid compositions are calculated in the sub-routine at line 460.

(3) Lines 210 and 270 calculate the progressive stages of the solidification and print the composition of the solid just formed, the average composition of the solid, the proportion of alloy that is solid and the composition of the liquid that remains. At line 260 a test is made and if the current temperature is below the eutectic temperature the solidification ends.

(4) Line 300 prints the range of solid compositions, the proportion of primary solid and the composition of the final eutectic solid which forms. In a micro-structure this will occur at the grain boundaries between the grains with the dendritic sub-structure.

(5) If the final solidification temperature is above the eutectic temperature lines 370–390 print the last liquid composition and the range of solid compositions.

Use of this program enables an appreciation to be obtained of the variation of composition in a typical chill cast alloy and indicates how this varies with the difference in solidus and liquidus temperatures for a given composition and shows under what circumstances eutectic solid may be expected in an alloy whose average composition is far from the eutectic composition. The simple assumptions that are made allow a reasonable simulation of the solidification process to be achieved.

Program 2.8: Quantitative metallography

```
90 REM 2.8 QUANTITATIVE METALLOGRAPHY
100 PAGE
110 PRINT "ENTER 1 FOR GRAIN SIZE ,2 FOR PARTICLES ";
120 INPUT A
```

```
130 PRINT
140 IF A=2 THEN 1000
150 IF A<>1 THEN 110
160 REM GRAIN SIZE FORMULAE
170 PRINT "ENTER LINE LENGTH mm.,NUMBER OF INTERCEPTS ";
180 INPUT L,N
190 PRINT
200 M=L/N
210 S=1+2*LOG(0.226/M)/LOG(2)
220 C=70/N^0.5
230 PRINT "Mean Linear Intercept =";M;"mm"
240 PRINT
250 PRINT "A.S.T.M. Grain Size =";S
260 PRINT
270 PRINT "95% Confidence limit =";C;"%"
280 PRINT
290 PRINT "Grain boundary area per mm^3 =";2/M;"mm^2"
300 GO TO 160
1000 REM PARTICLE FORMULAE
1010 PRINT "ENTER WIDTH OF FRAME IN PICTURE POINTS, mm. ";
1020 INPUT W1,W2
1030 PRINT "ENTER NUMBER OF LINES ";
1040 INPUT H
1050 PRINT
1060 PRINT "ENTER AREA,INTERCEPTS IN PICTURE POINTS ";
1070 INPUT A,I
1080 PRINT
1090 PRINT "ENTER NUMBER OF PARTICLES ";
1100 INPUT P
1110 PRINT
1120 PRINT "VOLUME FRACTION=";A/H/W1
1130 PRINT
1140 PRINT "MEAN PARTICLE SIZE=";A/I*W2/W1;"mm."
1150 PRINT
1160 PRINT "SURFACE/VOLUME RATIO=";4*I/A*W1/W2;"mm^-1"
1170 PRINT
1180 F=I^2/A/P
1190 PRINT "SHAPE FACTOR=";F;
1200 PRINT
1210 IF F>1.5 THEN 1350
1220 IF F<1 THEN 1320
1230 PRINT "REASONABLY UNIFORM SIZED SPHERES"
1240 PRINT
1250 PRINT "PARTICLES/UNIT VOLUME=";
1255 PRINT PI*P^2/4/I/H/W1*(W1/W2)^3;"mm^-3"
1260 PRINT
1270 PRINT "MEAN VOLUME OF PARTICLE=";
1275 PRINT 4*I*A/PI/P^2*(W2/W1)^3;"mm^3"
1280 PRINT
1290 PRINT "MEAN SURFACE AREA /PARTICLE=";
1295 PRINT 32/PI*(I*W2/P/W1)^2;"mm^2"
1300 PRINT
1310 GO TO 1370
1320 PRINT "NON-UNIFORM SIZES OR HORIZONTAL PARTICLES"
1330 PRINT
1340 GO TO 1370
1350 PRINT "REENTRANT OR TALL THIN PARTICLES"
1360 PRINT
1370 GO TO 1060
```

Program notes

(1) The grain structure is selected at line 110, the total length of line and total number of intercepts are requested at line 170.

(2) Line 200 calculates the mean linear intercept and line 210 calcu-

lates the ASTM grain size based on that mean linear intercept.
(3) Line 220 calculates the 95% confidence limit, which is dependent only on the number of intercepts that have been measured.
(4) These parameters are printed in lines 230–280 and in line 290 the grain boundary area per unit volume is printed which is simply twice the inverse of the mean linear intercept.
(5) The volume fraction of particles is calculated at line 1120, the mean particle size at line 1140 and the surface-to-volume ratio at line 1160. All these parameters are independent of the shape of the particles, and only depend on the analysis of the random line through a random plane section of the structure.
(6) The shape factor is calculated at line 1180 and for spherical particles of a uniform size, its value is $\frac{3}{8}\pi$ or 1.178.
(7) If the value of F is significantly different from this, no further calculation can be made, and so the program tests this at lines 1210 and 1220 and terminates at line 1370.
(8) If the particles are close to spherical in shape and of similar size, further analysis can be made and this is done at lines 1230–1300.

Normally this type of analysis would be built into the software associated with a quantitative microscope, but it is of interest to see the form of a simple program enabling the calculations to be made and the conversion for instance between mean linear intercept and ASTM grain size and the use of the shape factor to assess the validity of the 'uniform spheres' assumption.

PROBLEMS
(2.1) Program 2.1, as written, deals only with the most commonly met cubic crystal structures. It is quite possible to write a similar program for less symmetrical structures using the relevant, but more cumbersome, formulae. The present program requires that the crystal axes are at right-angles to each other, if this is not so, a totally new program must be written.

The reader might wish to study the case of a tetragonal structure where two of the dimensions of the unit cell are equal and the third is different. In this case the (110) plane will not appear the same as the (101) plane. All the z coordinates will have to be increased by a factor of c/a and the criterion for intersection becomes

$$xh + yk + zl\,c/a = 0$$

The polar coordinates used in lines 950 and 960 need only the modification that every value of C is multiplied by c/a.
(2.2) (Program 2.1) In assessing crystal planes the density of packing of atoms on a plane is important. This is simply the number of atoms per unit area of the plane. The planes with the highest pack-

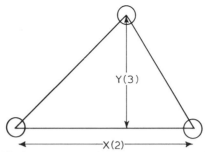

Figure 2.13 Diagram representing the coordinates required for the circulation of density of packing of a plane of atoms

ing density are normally the planes on which deformation occurs. An element of the packing arrangement of atoms is a triangle based on the origin as shown in Figure 2.13. The number of atoms contained within the triangle is one half, since the sum of the angles within the triangle is 180°. The area of the triangle is 1/2 × X(2) × Y(3) so the density of packing is the inverse of X(2) × Y(3). Modify Program 2.1 to include this calculation.

It is possible that another atom will be closer to the line joining the origin and atom 2 than atom 3 is. Write a further modification of Program 2.1 that will allow for this.

(2.3) If Program 2.1 is to be used to index electron diffraction patterns then the indices or coordinates of each atom need to be printed next to its position. Modify Program 2.1 to do this.

(2.4) As an addition to the simple series of programs given (Program 2.2), the reader may wish to include the simple relationship governing the stress required to bow a dislocation out between two obstacles a distance, d, apart on the slip plane. The shear stress, T, required is given by the formula

$$T = Gb/d$$

where G = modulus of rigidity and b = Burgers vector.

(2.5) (Program 2.2) Because there is a stress acting on edge dislocations on parallel slip planes they align themselves one above the other and so generate a tilt boundary. The angle of tilt, θ, is related to the vertical separation of the dislocations h by the formula

$$\theta = \frac{b}{h}$$

This calculation can also be added to the original program (Program 2.2) very easily.

(2.6) As written, Program 2.3 will only plot the position of pole (hkl) if l is not negative. Modify the program so that if l is negative the pole $(-h, -k, -l)$ is plotted.

(2.7) (Program 2.3) It can be useful to know the angle that a given pole makes with the cube directions [100], [010] and [001]. The three angles are usually referred to as α, β and γ respectively and are given by the formula

$$\cos \alpha = \frac{h}{\sqrt{h^2 + k^2 + l^2}}$$

$$\cos \beta = \frac{k}{\sqrt{h^2 + k^2 + l^2}}$$

$$\cos \gamma = \frac{l}{\sqrt{h^2 + k^2 + l^2}}$$

Modify Program 2.3 so that these angles are printed for each pole plotted.

(2.8) It can also be of great value to know the angle the pole (h,k,l) makes with a given pole (u,v,w). Modify the original Program 2.3 so that (u,v,w) can be entered and the angle printed from the formula

$$\cos \theta = \frac{hu + kv + lw}{(h^2 + k^2 + u^2)(u^2 + v^2 + w^2)}$$

(2.9) (Program 2.3) Problems may arise in which there is a requirement to plot the trace of the (h,k,l) plane as well as the (h,k,l) pole. This can be done by constructing an arc of, say, 20 linear elements going from the position of pole $(-k,h,0)$ through $(-hl,kl,h^2 + k^2)$ to $(k,-h,0)$. This increases the length of the program (Program 2.3) but does enable problems involving intersecting planes to be solved graphically.

(2.10) In order to limit the data input to such a program (Program 2.4), the atomic weights of all the elements could be stored as part of the program and called on during the operation of the program. Suggest a way in which the elements could be indicated so that the correct atomic weight could be selected from the list of those contained within a data statement in the program. This kind of facility is written into Program 4.1.

(2.11) As written, Program 2.4 requires that the values of weight percent or atomic percent entered should sum to 100%. Often, the most abundant element is calculated by balance, i.e. 100% less the sum of the other elements. Rewrite Program 2.4 so that the final element entered is determined by balance.

(2.12) Program 2.5 could be extended to cover intermediate phases. There are size factor, electrochemical and electron concentration requirements which indicate the formation of a large number of the different types of intermediate compounds and these could also be included in a program of the type shown. Size factor differences of greater than 14% have been seen to lead to restricted primary solubility, but larger size differences give particular types of intermetallic compound. 20% to 30% size differences occur in Laves phases although size difference is not the only criterion for their formation. Size ratios greater than 0.59 lead to complex structures such as that of Fe_3C but size ratios in the range 0.41 to 0.59 give rise to interstitial compounds of simple structure such as TiC which has the NaCl structure. Size ratios less than 0.41 occur in interstitial solid solutions.

Electrochemical compounds are more difficult to predict as although stable compounds such as Mg_2Si arise from atoms with a large difference in electro-negativity, other factors are also important. Covalent compounds where the sum of the valence electrons is 8, such as ZnS and AlN, can be predicted but these are not strictly intermetallic compounds. Electron compounds, which occur in alloys of monovalent metals at electron atom ratios of 3/2, 21/13 and 7/4, can obviously be predicted fairly easily certainly in Cu, Ag and Au alloys.

(2.13) (Program 2.5) The original formulation of the Hume–Rothery rules applied only to non-transition metals. Barrett[2] has summarized development of the rules to the study of nickel based super alloys. To overcome the problem of valency electrons of a transition metal, the Pauling Electron Vacancy Number of each element is used. This is referred to as N and in almost every case is given by the formula

$$N = 10.66 - F$$

where F is the total number of electrons outside the last stable configuration.

Chromium has an electron structure of $1s^2\ 2s^2\ 2p^6\ 3s^2\ 3p^6\ 3d^5\ 4s^1$ and so has six electrons outside the last stable configuration of argon which is $1s^1\ 2s^2\ 2p^6\ 3s^2\ 3p^6$. The electron valency number N for chromium therefore is 4.66.

The weight average value of this electron vacancy number for the matrix of a super alloy after precipitation indicates the susceptibility of the alloy to the formation of sigma phase in service. If the weight average value of N is less than 2.5 the alloy is free from the formation of sigma phase. An assessment of this type can be very valuable since sigma phase only develops over very long periods of time and so laboratory testing for the formation of sigma phase is extremely laborious and time consuming. A simple calculation of the type proposed by Barrett is a very rewarding short cut for the alloy developer. The reader may wish to write a program allowing for the calculation of the weight average value of N for the matrix of a super alloy containing Cr, Mo, W, Ti, Nb, V, Ta and Zr. In order to determine the composition of the matrix it is necessary to account for the removal of all the elements contained in the carbides and the γ precipitate.

(2.14) The equilibrium cooling sequence of a given alloy is often of interest. It involves determination of the condition of an alloy of given composition through a progression of reducing temperatures. Program 2.6 can easily be modified to do this by undertaking a repeat series of calculations at a given value of B but for progressively decreasing values of S. The steps in S could be 20 terminating at room temperature, or the program could be written so that the step size can be specified.

(2.15) Instead of using the seven fixed points included in the data statement on lines 160, modify the initial part of Program 2.6 to allow for values of temperature and composition of the fixed points to be input prior to the use of the program. It will be necessary to have a diagram similar to that shown in Figure 2.12 for the particular fixed points supplied, otherwise the educational value of the program will be largely lost. The phase boundaries used in this program are all linear and are given by the formula in line 920. Some other simple shape could be used for the phase boundary formula. How much modification to the program would be required if some formula other than a linear one were incorporated?

(2.16) To obviate the necessity of providing a diagram such as Figure 2.12 the equilibrium diagram could be drawn on the VDU screen. Write an element of Program 2.6 that allows the diagram to be drawn from the fixed points $T(I)$ and $C(I)$.

(2.17) (Program 2.7) At first sight it might be assumed that the cooling rate would be constant, but due to the evolution of the latent heat of fusion that is not so. The time interval between each of the twenty stages of solidification can be written as

$$t = \frac{A(T1 - T2) + B(P(1) - P(2))}{C}$$

where A, B and C are constants and $P(1)$ and $P(2)$ are the proportions solidified in successive intervals. The reader can introduce this time interval into the program using, say, $A=1$, $B=20$, $C=20$ to give some indication of the progress of solidification with time.

(2.18) (Program 2.8) When dealing with a grain structure the 95% confidence limit can be calculated from the number of intercepts only. However, for a particle structure it is necessary to analyse a number of frames before such a confidence limit can be calculated. If a parameter x is measured n times and the resulting average value is $\bar{x}$ with a standard deviation of σ, there is a 95% chance that the true value of x will lie between $x + 2\,(\sigma/n)$ and $x - 2\,(\sigma/n)$. Modify the particle part of Program 2.8 to analyse a series of frames, to calculate the standard deviation of volume fraction and mean particle size and to print the 95% confidence limits on these two parameters. **(2.19)** (Program 2.8) If very large grain structures are specified the ASTM grain size becomes negative which is clearly not satisfactory. Calculate at what value of mean linear intercept this occurs and introduce a criterion into the program which rejects data leading to negative ASTM grain sizes.

References

(1) Pritchard, H. O. and Skinner, H. A., *Chem. Rev.*, **55**, 745, (1955).
(2) Barrett, C. S., *J. Inst. Metals*, **100**, 65–73, (1972).

Bibliography

Van Vlack, L. H., *Materials Science for Engineers*, Addison Wesley, (1982).
Ashby, M. F. and Jones, D. R. H., *Engineering Materials, an Introduction to their Properties and Applications*, Pergamon, (1980).
Cottrell, A. H., *Introduction to Metallurgy*, Arnold, (1975).
Cullity, B. D., *Elements of X-Ray Diffraction*, Addison Wesley, (1978).
Pickering, F. B., *The Basis of Quantitative Metallography*, Inst. of Metallurgical Technicians, (1976).

Chapter 3

Thermodynamics and kinetics of solids

ESSENTIAL THEORY

3.1 Introduction

There are two principal approaches to the physical chemistry of solids. The first, thermodynamics, answers the question 'what is the position of equilibrium for a reaction?' It can be used to predict whether an oxide ore can be reduced to a metal by carbon, and to determine the equilibrium concentration of vacancies in a crystalline solid as a function of temperature. The second, kinetics, answers the question 'how fast does the reaction proceed?' It can be used to determine the rate of corrosion of iron in water, or the rate of decarburization of liquid iron in an oxygen converter.

To solve a problem using thermodynamics requires no knowledge of the path that the reaction undergoes, and, in many cases, a knowledge of the behaviour of atoms is not necessary. A mechanical analogy may be used to illustrate this. Consider a billiard table that has one corner lower than the other three. If a ball is played, it will finish in the lowest corner, since there it will have the lowest potential energy. It is not necessary to determine the route the ball takes from its initial position to its final position; provided that the ball is hit hard enough to overcome friction, it will arrive at the lowest corner. For a chemical reaction the final equilibrium will be when the free energy is a minimum. In the case of solids at a constant pressure, usually 1 atmosphere the free energy is the Gibbs free energy, G.

For reactions of solids and liquids close to their melting point, kinetics will include the rates of transport of reactants to reaction sites and products away from reaction sites, as well as the kinetics of the chemical reaction at the reaction site. Thus, many problems in the kinetics of reactions in metallurgy and materials science reduce to problems in diffusion or, if liquids are involved, fluid mechanics.

An example to show how the thermodynamic and kinetic approaches can be used is the behaviour of aluminium and its oxide.

Aluminium oxide (alumina) is very stable, with a free energy of formation of 1580 kJ/mole at 298K. Thermodynamics shows that alumina cannot be reduced to aluminium by carbon at temperatures below 2300 K, and therefore aluminium metal is produced by the electrolysis of alumina.

Aluminium oxide is more stable than aluminium metal, yet is often used unpainted in contact with air. Kinetics show how this is possible. When the aluminium is in contact with air, a thin layer of aluminium oxide is produced. For the reaction to continue, it is necessary for aluminium to migrate by diffusion through the aluminium oxide. This diffusion at room temperature is very slow, and so aluminium can be used in air unpainted. Indeed, in more corrosive environments, the aluminium oxide film can be artificially thickened by anodizing and the rate of corrosion is slowed, compared to that for unanodized aluminium with its thinner oxide film.

3.2 Thermodynamic relationships

The enthalpy, H, of a system at constant pressure may be defined as the sum of the internal energy, E, of the system and the work done by the system on the surroundings, PV

$$H = E + PV \qquad (3.1)$$

Alternatively, the enthalpy can be related to the Gibbs free energy, G, the temperature, T, and the entropy, S

$$G = H - TS \qquad (3.2)$$

therefore

$$H = G + TS \qquad (3.3)$$

The above relationships are shown diagrammatically in Figure 3.1

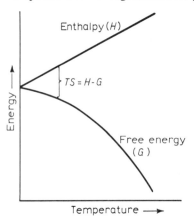

Figure 3.1 Enthalpy — free energy relationship

For a substance which does not change its state, e.g. α-iron or liquid tin, the enthalpy increases with temperature, according to Equation (3.4).

$$H_2 = H_1 + \int_{T_1}^{T_2} C_p \, dT \qquad (3.4)$$

where H_1 and H_2 are the enthalpies at temperatures T_1 and T_2 and C_p the heat capacity (specific heat) at constant pressure. For many solids, the heat capacity may be expressed as a function of temperature, K.

$$C_p = a + bT - \frac{c}{T^2} \qquad (3.5)$$

Values of a, b and c for many substances have been determined[1].

For solids, it is easier to measure the heat capacity at constant pressure C_p than the heat capacity at constant volume C_v. Normally, if the heat capacity of a solid at constant volume C_v is required, it is derived from a knowledge of more easily measured quantities using Equation (3.6).

$$C_p = C_v + \frac{\alpha^2 VT}{\beta} \qquad (3.6)$$

where α = volume coefficient of thermal expansion, β = volume coefficient of compressibility, V = volume and T = temperature. As a first approximation for solids at temperatures above the Debye temperature, i.e. above 300 K, C_p and C_v can be taken as equal.

3.3 Rates of reaction — the Arrhenius equation

Arrhenius (1859–1927) observed that the rate at which a chemical reaction proceeded was strongly dependent on temperature and formulated the following equation which has subsequently been shown to hold for a wide variety of reactions and transformations

$$\text{Rate} = A \exp(-Q/RT) \qquad (3.7)$$

where A is a constant, Q is the activation energy and T is the absolute temperature.

The activation energy is the energy that must be supplied in order that a reaction might proceed. This may be usefully illustrated by a mechanical analogue, as shown in Figure 3.2. When the block is in Position 1, its potential energy, $E_1 = mgh_1$. In Position 3 its potential energy, E_3, is lower and = mgh_3. Thus, in going from Position 1 to Position 3, an energy of $-mg(h_1 - h_3)$ is released. (The negative sign shows that energy is released to the surroundings.)

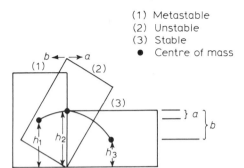

Figure 3.2 Activation energy — mechanical analogue.
Note: (a) corresponds to activation energy required to go from the metastable to the stable situation. (b) corresponds to activation required to go from the stable to metastable position, considerably greater than (a)

However, the movement from Position 1 to Position 3 cannot occur spontaneously. Energy must be supplied to raise the block to position 2 before it can fall to Position 3. This energy supplied is mg $(h_2 - h_1)$, and represents the activation energy required to permit the block to go from Position 1 to Position 3. Similarly, for a chemical reaction, energy must be supplied to the reactants to form an activated complex which then decomposes to form the products of reaction.

3.4 Diffusion

Atoms in solids are free to move and this movement increases exponentially with temperature. Figure 3.3(a) illustrates the process of self-diffusion. A surface of a solid is coated with a

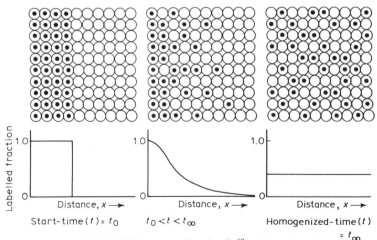

Figure 3.3 Self-diffusion — radioactive Co^{60} on the surface of non-radioactive cobalt

radioactive isotope of the same element as the solid, e.g. Co^{60} on a cobalt block. The isotope will diffuse into the block and the concentration profiles of the radioactive atoms are shown as a function of time in Figures 3.3(b), (c), (d).

The net flux of diffusing atoms is proportional to the concentration gradient

$$J = - D \frac{dc}{dx} \qquad (3.8)$$

where J = flux in moles/unit area/unit time (moles/m²/s), D = diffusion coefficient (m²/s) and dc/dx = concentration gradient (moles/m⁴). Equation (3.8) is known as Fick's first law. The diffusion coefficient increases exponentially with temperature (Equation (3.9)), and is a function of composition.

$$D = D_0 \exp\left(-E_D/RT\right) \qquad (3.9)$$

where E_D is the activation energy for diffusion.

The activation energy for diffusion for crystalline solids can be explained as a combination of the energy required for an atom to leave its lattice site and to move to another vacant lattice site.

Note that Equation (3.9) is used several times in Program 5.1 as well as other programs involving diffusion.

Fick's first law applies for steady-state diffusion, such as the diffusion of a gas through a metal membrane. If the concentration of a diffusing species at a particular point varies with time, such as in Figure 3.3 or for the diffusion of carbon in γ-iron during the carburizing process, it is necessary to use Fick's second law (Equation (3.10)). For one-dimensional diffusion, Fick's second law can be stated as

$$\frac{\partial C}{\partial t} = \frac{\partial}{\partial x}\left(D \frac{\partial C}{\partial x}\right) \qquad (3.10)$$

If D is regarded as independent of concentration, Equation (3.10) can be written as

$$\frac{\partial C}{\partial t} = D\left(\frac{\partial^2 C}{\partial x^2}\right) \qquad (3.11)$$

3.5 Analysis of resistivity data

Many different parameters would provide suitable monitors for determining the kinetics of reactions. Electrical conductivity, chosen in this instance, proves particularly suitable for the investigation of kinetics in precipitation hardening systems.

The electrical conductivity of a pure metal is least affected by alloying additions when they exist as a precipitated second phase. It is, therefore, convenient to monitor the changes in electrical conductivity occurring during the aging of solution annealed alloys and to use them to determine reaction velocities and to provide the basis for further analysis.

Families of sigmoidal decay curves are produced when the resistivity is plotted against the logarithm of the aging time for experiments conducted at different temperatures. The time taken to a certain fraction transformed may then be plotted against the reciprocal of the aging temperature to determine the empirical activation energy (see Equation (3.7)).

Further information regarding the transformation kinetics may be obtained by treatment of the resistivity data after Johnson and Mehl[2]

$$Y = 1 - \exp\left(-\,(kt)^n\right) \qquad (3.12)$$

where Y is the fraction transformed, k is the rate constant, t the time and n the time exponent.

An equivalent form of Equation (3.12) is

$$\ln\left(\frac{1}{1-Y}\right) = (kt)^n \qquad (3.13)$$

Converting to common logarithms and taking logarithms again produces,

$$\log.\log\left(\frac{1}{1-Y}\right) = n \log t + n \log k - \log 2.3 \qquad (3.14)$$

Hence, if a reaction conforms to the Johnson–Mehl equation, a graph of $\log.\log\left(\frac{1}{1-Y}\right)$ against log time will be linear. The value of the time exponent, n, is obtained from the slope of such a plot and may take any positive value, but the range most commonly encountered is 0.5–2.5. Burke[3] has listed a selection of values for

Table 3.1

Model	n
Diffusion controlled growth of a fixed number of particles	3/2
Growth of a fixed number of particles limited by the interface process	3
Diffusion controlled growth of cylinders in axial direction only	1
Diffusion controlled growth of discs of constant thickness	2
Growth of dislocations	2/3
Nucleation at a constant rate and diffusion controlled growth	5/2
Growth of a fixed number of eutectoid cells	3
Nucleation at a constant rate and growth of a eutectoid	4

the time exponent, n, which have been derived from this type of transformation, collected from many workers, notably Avrami and has described the various transformation models the values are found to represent. Some values of n with a description of associated models are shown in Table 3.1. The equation produces accurate solutions for n up to values of 40% reaction.

3.6 Shear transformations (martensitic reactions)

Not all reactions are diffusion controlled but instead take place by the cooperative displacement of atoms in a shear-like manner. This is true of the polymorphic transformation in cobalt which may be summarized thus

$$Co\,(fcc) \xrightarrow[1120°C]{Cooling} Co\,(hcp) \qquad (3.15)$$

The {111} planes of the face-centred-cubic (fcc) high tempera-ture phase are stacked ABCABC . . . whilst the {001} planes of the low temperature hexagonal-close-packed (hcp) phase are stacked ABABAB . . . . The planes of the two structures are identical, both being close-packed, and the high temperature phase may thus achieve the low temperature form by the C layer of the fcc structure moving by part of an atomic distance to produce the hcp stacking. Shear processes of this type may be induced by super-cooling, mechanical stress or a combination of the two.

A further example of this type of transformation, which has great engineering significance, is the austenite to martensite transforma-tion in carbon-containing steels

$$\gamma\,(\text{austenite fcc}) \xrightarrow[M_s - M_f]{Cooling} \text{Martensite (bct)} \qquad (3.16)$$

where the transformation takes place over a temperature range, starting at M_s and finishing at M_f. In pure iron the change would be from a fcc to a body-centred-cubic (bcc) structure, but in carbon-containing steels the enforced solution of the interstitial carbon dis-torts the low-temperature form to body-centred-tetragonal (bct).

The importance of martensite lies, not so much in its extremely high hardness, but in the excellent combination of strength, ductil-ity and transition temperature which may be achieved by judicious tempering of the martensite structure. It is, therefore, important that it should be possible to produce martensite in thick sections to optimize the properties of large engineering components. Martensite in simple carbon steels can only be produced by very rapid cooling; however, the hardenability (thickness through which full hardening is possible) may be improved by metallic alloying additions.

Many attempts have been made to produce empirical mathematical relationships to enable calculation of hardenability from data on the elements commonly used as additions to steels. A recent paper by Deb et al.[4] expresses the ideal critical diameter (hardenability) D_I as a product of polynomials in carbon and alloy content

$$D_I = D_I^0 \prod_i f_i(X_i) \qquad (3.17)$$

where D_I^0 is the base diameter (determined by grain size and carbon content) and f is a multiplying factor due to an alloying element.

For homogeneous low- and medium-carbon steels of a given grain size, Equation (3.13) may be rewritten

$$D_I = D_I^0 \prod_i f_i(X_i) \qquad (3.18)$$

where D_I^0 is the ideal critical diameter of an unalloyed steel of given grain size and is a function of its carbon content x_c, and x_i is the concentration of alloying element i in weight percentage. The functions D_I^0 and f_i are expressed in power series as

$$D_I^0 = \sum_j b_{cj} X_c^j \qquad (3.19)$$

$$f_i = \sum_j a_{ij} X_i^j \qquad (3.20)$$

where j is a positive integer including zero. By combining Equations (3.18–3.20) and substituting appropriate coefficients, the hardenability of any low- or medium-carbon steel may be calculated from

$$D_I = \left(\sum_j b_{cj} X_c^j\right) \prod_i \left(\sum_j a_{ij} X_i^j\right) \qquad (3.21)$$

The grain size dependence and composition limits over which the various coefficients apply are indicated in Tables 3.2 and 3.3.

3.7 Corrosion

Corrosion and its prevention remains a very significant problem in the engineering industry. Electrochemical corrosion of metals, where a metal in contact with an electrolyte, usually water, is a very common form of corrosion. Studying corrosion involves the use of thermodynamics (which corrodes when copper and zinc are connected in water?) and kinetics (will this steel sheet corrode through in 1 month or 20 years?).

To determine which electrode in a particular electrochemical cell

Table 3.2 Coefficients b_{cj} and a_{ij} for use in Equation (3.17) for calculating hardenability of low-carbon steels (0.15–0.25%C)

j	b_{cj}				a_{ij}					
	GS6	GS7	GS8	GS9	Si	Mn	Cr	Mo	Ni	Mo with >1.0% Ni
0	0.0342	0.0337	0.02772	0.0252	1.0020	0.9940	1.0568	0.9908	1.0033	1.6360
1	2.1774	2.0143	1.9488	1.7880	0.0071	0.6605	−0.6407	1.1960	−0.0105	−1.1390
2	−1.5000	−1.333	−1.4048	−1.1905	−0.1994	1.9863	5.3626	1.0489	1.1255	3.399
3	:	:	:	:	0.3802	−1.2143	−7.0685	−0.2348	−1.3864	:
4	:	:	:	:	−0.1091	0.2868	4.1646	:	0.7540	:
5	:	:	:	:	:	:	−0.7779	:	−0.1862	:
6	:	:	:	:	:	:	:	:	0.0175	:
Composition limits over which the coefficients are valid	$0.15 < X_C < 0.25$				$0.01 < X_{Si}$ < 2.0	$0.01 < X_{Mn}$ < 1.4	$0.01 < X_{Cr}$ < 1.65	$0.01 < X_{Mn}$ < 1.0	$0.01 < X_{Si}$ < 3.75	$0.65 < X_{Mo}$ < 1.0

Table 3.3 Coefficients b_{cj} and a_{ij} for use in Equation (3.17) for calculating hardenability of medium-carbon steels (0.25–0.60%C)

j	b_{cj}				a_{ij}							
	GS5	GS6	GS7	GS8	Si	Mn	Mn	Cr	Mo	Mo	Ni	Cu
0	−0.1552	−0.1448	−0.1190	−0.1638	0.9949	0.9954	−3.5600	0.9802	0.9761	1.5096	0.9834	0.9938
1	3.7559	3.5441	3.2617	3.4224	0.5215	0.4650	7.1700	2.0060	2.4060	−5.4570	1.7184	1.6343
2	−4.7143	−4.5003	−4.2499	−4.7499	−0.6969	−0.4136	−2.6700	−1.9313	−1.3661	−4.7053	−1.3489	−1.5615
3	2.1296	2.0373	2.0369	2.4074	0.6173	0.6029	0.4610	3.4874	0.4996	−7.5578	0.3050	0.7876
4	⋮	⋮	⋮	⋮	−0.1368	⋮	⋮	−2.5915	⋮	⋮	0.0731	−0.1442
5	⋮	⋮	⋮	⋮	⋮	⋮	⋮	0.8537	⋮	⋮	−0.0240	⋮
6	⋮	⋮	⋮	⋮	⋮	⋮	⋮	−0.1034	⋮	⋮	⋮	⋮
Composition limits over which the coefficients are valid	$0.25 < X_C < 0.6$				$0.01 < X_{Si}$ <2.0	$0.01 < X_{Mn}$ <1.2	$1.2 < X_{Mn}$ <2.5	$0.01 < X_{Cr}$ <2.8	$0.01 < X_{Mo}$ <0.65	$0.65 < X_{Mo}$ <1.0	$0.01 < X_{Ni}$ <3.0	$0.01 < X_{Cu}$ <2.0

is the anode and, therefore, will corrode, involves the use of the Nernst equation. For the electrode reaction

$$M^{z+} + ze^- \rightarrow M \tag{3.22}$$

the potential is given by

$$E = E^0 - \frac{RT}{zF}\ln\frac{a_M}{a_M^{z+}} \tag{3.23}$$

where E = potential; E^0 = standard electrode potential, where M is in its standard state, e.g. Zn at 298 K would be as solid, and the electrolyte is at unit activity; a_M = activity of metal M. This will be defined as 1 for the pure metal. For an alloy, $a_M = \gamma_M N_M$ where γ_M is the activity coefficient of M and N_M is the atom M fraction M in the alloy; a_M^{z+} = activity of metal ions (M^{z+}). This will equal $\gamma_M^{z+} C_M^{z+}$ for dilute solutions, where γ_M^{z+} = activity coefficient of M^{z+} ions and C_M^{z+} = concentration of M^{z+} ions. As $C_M^{z+} \rightarrow 0$, $\gamma_M^{z+} \rightarrow 1$, i.e. as solution becomes infinitely dilute the activity of the iron will equal its concentration; R = universal gas constant; T = temperature (K) and F = the faraday (96,487 C/mole). For two electrodes connected together, the cell voltage may be calculated from

$$E = E_C - E_A \tag{3.24}$$

where E_C = potential of cathode and E_A = potential of anode both calculated from Equation (3.23).

Calculations of this type indicate whether an electrode will be an anode and corrode. It will tell us nothing about the current flowing through the cell, and, therefore, nothing about the rate of corrosion. To calculate rates of corrosion, it is necessary to consider the rates of transport of reactants to the electrode, the rates of reaction at the electrode and the rate of transport of products away from the electrode.

PROGRAMS

Program 3.1: Calculation of activation energy – diffusion of Cu in CuO.

The program is designed to accept data from experiments on the oxidation of copper conducted at a series of temperatures. From the experimental data the program calculates the empirical activation energy for self diffusion of copper based on the implementation of the Arrhenius rate equation, (Equation (3.7)). Table 3.4 presents data from a series of such experiments which should be used in running the program.

Table 3.4

Material: Copper
Area of samples used: 132.74 mm^2
Results: Weight increase in grams for times at given temperatures

Temperature (°C) Time (min)	462	579	793	932
60	0.000035	0.000095	0.00071	0.00260
120	0.000060	0.000140	0.00086	0.00315
180	0.000080	0.000170	0.00098	0.00360
240	0.000095	0.000195	0.00110	0.00390
300	0.000110	0.000220	0.00120	0.00415
360	0.00120	0.000250	0.00130	0.00440
420	0.000135	0.000265	0.00142	0.00460

Explanation of oxidation mechanism

Metal oxides are not normally stoichiometric. In the copper oxidation reaction above 400°C the growing film of cuprous oxide absorbs oxygen to build up new layers of the oxide with the corresponding formation of vacant cation sites (Cu^+) or $+$ and divalent cupric ions Cu^{2+}, by convention represented as electron vacancies, or 'holes' ⓔ. The reaction may be written

$$2\,Cu + \tfrac{1}{2}O_2 \rightarrow Cu_2O + 2\,\boxed{+} + 2\,ⓔ \qquad (3.25)$$

two cation vacancies and two positive holes being formed for each oxygen atom absorbed.

The oxidation then proceeds if the external pressure of O_2 > the dissociation pressure of Cu_2O, with cation vacancies and positive holes created at the $Cu_2O/O_2(g)$ interface and moving inwards to be destroyed at the $Cu_{(m)}/Cu_2O$ interface as more Cu ions enter the Cu_2O lattice. Thus the Cu_2O behaves as a p-type semi-conductor.

$$Cu^+ \qquad Cu^+ \qquad \qquad Cu^+$$
$$\qquad O^{2-} \qquad \quad O^{2-} \qquad O^{2-} \qquad O^{2-}$$
$$Cu^+ \qquad Cu^{2-} \qquad Cu^+ \qquad Cu^+$$

The proposed mechanism would suggest that the rate of increase in thickness of the oxidized layer might be given by

$$dx/dt = A/x \qquad (3.26)$$

where x is the thickness of the film and A is a constant. Integrating leads to

$$x^2 = Kt + K^1 \qquad (3.27)$$

where K represents $2A$ and K^1 is the integration constant.

Thus we can write the rate equation in terms of Δm, the increase in weight per unit area, k_p, the rate constant and C another constant as

$$(\Delta m)^2 = k_p t + C \tag{3.28}$$

Now as the growth of the oxide layer is controlled by the inter-related transport of holes and vacancies, then the rate constant, k_p, is proportional to the coefficient of self diffusion of Cu^+ in Cu_2O, i.e. D^O where D^O is a function of temperature.

$$D^O = B \exp\left(-Q/kT\right) \tag{3.29}$$

where Q is an energy barrier to diffusion and k is Boltzman's constant (B is also a constant). Thus we may say

$$k_p = m \exp\left(-\frac{Q}{RT}\right) \tag{3.30}$$

where Q is the activation energy of self diffusion of Cu^+ in Cu_2O, R is the gas constant and m is another constant.

```
100  INIT
110  PAGE
120  REM 3.1 CALCN OF ACTIVATION ENERGY-DIFF.OF Cu IN CuO
150  PRINT "ENTER NUMBER OF TIMES TO BE PROCESSED"
160  INPUT Z
170  DIM T1(Z),W(Z+1),A(Z),X1(Z),Y1(Z)
180  PRINT "ENTER NUMBER OF TEMPERATURES USED IN EXPERIMENT"
190  INPUT K2
200  K3=K2
210  DIM K1(K2),M1(K2+1),R1(K2+1)
220  PRINT "ENTER AREA OF SAMPLES USED IN mm^2"
230  INPUT M5
240  PRINT "ENTER TIMES IN SECS IN ASCENDING ORDER"
250  INPUT T1
260  I1=0
270  PRINT
280  PRINT
290  PRINT
300  PRINT "ENTER WEIGHT IN GRAMS AT EACH TIME -INCREASING"
310  PRINT "TIME ORDER followed by TEMP OF EXPT IN oC"
320  INPUT W
330  FOR I=1 TO Z
340  A(I)=(W(I)/M5)^2
350  X1(I)=T1(I)
360  Y1(I)=A(I)
370  NEXT I
380  GOSUB 1000
390  I1=I1+1
400  K1(I1)=W(Z+1)
410  M1(I1)=LOG(M)
420  R1(I1)=R
430  K3=K3-1
440  IF K3<>0 THEN 270
450  FOR I3=1 TO 500
460  NEXT I3
470  DELETE X1,Y1,Z
480  DIM X1(K2),Y1(K2)
490  Z=K2
500  FOR I=1 TO K2
510  X1(I)=1/(K1(I)+273)
```

```
520 Y1(I)=M1(I)
530 NEXT I
540 GOSUB 1000
550 PAGE
560 PRINT "TEMP OF EXPT oC      LGN SLOPE          CORREL.COEF"
570 FOR I=1 TO K2
580 PRINT K1(I),M1(I),R1(I)
590 NEXT I
600 PRINT
610 PRINT "**********************************************"
620 PRINT
630 PRINT
640 PRINT "ACTIVATION ENERGY=",ABS(M*8.3143/1000),"KJ/MOL/K"
650 PRINT
660 PRINT "CORREL.COEF.=",R
670 END
1000 REM TO PLOT BEST STRAIGHT LINE THROUGH POINTS
1010 DELETE X,N,Y,C,L
1020 N=Z
1030 DIM X(N+7),Y(N+7)
1040 FOR I=1 TO Z
1050 X(I)=X1(I)
1060 Y(I)=Y1(I)
1070 NEXT I
1080 E1=0
1090 E2=0
1100 E3=0
1110 E4=0
1120 E5=0
1130 FOR I=1 TO N
1140 E1=E1+X(I)
1150 E2=E2+X(I)*X(I)
1160 E3=E3+Y(I)
1170 E4=E4+Y(I)*Y(I)
1180 E5=E5+X(I)*Y(I)
1190 NEXT I
1200 M=(E5-E1*E3/N)/(E2-E1*E1/N)
1210 C=(E1*E5-E3*E2)/(E1*E1-N*E2)
1220 S=((E2-E1*E1/N)*(E4-E3*E3/N))^0.5
1230 R=(E5-E1*E3/N)/S
1240 K=((E4-E3*E3/N-M*R*S)/(N-2))^0.5
1250 REM SELECT VALUE OF T
1260 IF N-2=1 THEN 1460
1270 IF N-2=2 THEN 1480
1280 IF N-2=3 THEN 1500
1290 IF N-2=4 THEN 1520
1300 IF N-2=5 THEN 1540
1310 IF N-2=6 THEN 1560
1320 IF N-2=7 THEN 1580
1330 IF N-2=8 THEN 1600
1340 IF N-2=9 THEN 1620
1350 IF N-2=10 THEN 1640
1360 IF N-2<13 THEN 1660
1370 IF N-2<16 THEN 1680
1380 IF N-2<21 THEN 1700
1390 IF N-2<25 THEN 1720
1400 IF N-2<31 THEN 1740
1410 IF N-2<41 THEN 1760
1420 IF N-2<61 THEN 1780
1430 IF N-2<121 THEN 1800
1440 T=1.96
1450 GO TO 1810
1460 T=12.71
1470 GO TO 1810
1480 T=4.3
1490 GO TO 1810
1500 T=3.18
1510 GO TO 1810
1520 T=2.78
```

```
1530 GO TO 1810
1540 T=2.57
1550 GO TO 1810
1560 T=2.45
1570 GO TO 1810
1580 T=2.36
1590 GO TO 1810
1600 T=2.31
1610 GO TO 1810
1620 T=2.26
1630 GO TO 1810
1640 T=2.23
1650 GO TO 1810
1660 T=2.18
1670 GO TO 1810
1680 T=2.13
1690 GO TO 1810
1700 T=2.09
1710 GO TO 1810
1720 T=2.06
1730 GO TO 1810
1740 T=2.04
1750 GO TO 1810
1760 T=2.02
1770 GO TO 1810
1780 T=2
1790 GO TO 1810
1800 T=1.98
1810 U=M+K*T*(N/(N*E2-E1*E1))^0.5
1820 L=2*M-U
1830 PRINT
1840 IF K3=0 THEN 1880
1850 PAGE
1860 PRINT "FOR EXPT. AT TEMPERATURE oC",W(Z+1)
1870 PRINT "SLOPE =",M,"CORREL.COEF.=",R
1880 RETURN
```

Program notes

(1) The value entered as 'the number of times to be processed' in line 160 is used to dimension storage arrays in line 170. The array W is extended by 1 to $(Z + 1)$ to provide space for the temperature of the experiment in addition to the weights, all the data being entered at line 320. In similar fashion K2 in line 190 is used to dimension arrays in line 210, two of these being extended by 1 as they are to store values of slopes and correlation coefficients, not just for initial plots of $(wt/\text{area})^2$ against time, but also for the final Arrhenius plot.

(2) The K3 in line 200 is to be used in conditional branching in line 430.

(3) Data entries common to all experimental temperatures are complete by line 250.

(4) The I1 put equal to zero in line 260 is used to position data in storage arrays, see lines 390–420.

(5) Calculation of $(wt/\text{area})^2$ is done within the FOR . . . NEXT loop, lines 330–370 together with the changing of data from arrays T1 and A to X1 and Y1 respectively as their names are used in the regression analysis sub-routine, lines 1000–1880, invoked in line 380.

(6) On return from sub-routine 1000 data necessary for the final Arrhenius plot is massaged and stored together with information required in final output.

(7) Lines 430–450 determine conditional branching. If data on further temperatures is to be entered the program branches back to line 270 whilst if all runs are complete the program progresses and calculates the activation energy. This is done in lines 470–540 again using sub-routine 1000 after changing data locations as necessary.

(8) Final output is achieved in lines 550–670.

(9) The linear regression, sub-routine 1000, determines slope M in line 1200, intercept C in line 1210, correlation coefficient R in line 1230 and the standard deviation K in line 1240. The upper and lower limits for the slope, U and L respectively, are determined via selected T values at lines 1810 and 1820.

Program 3.2: Calculation of reaction times from activation energy

Knowing a value for the activation energy of a particular process and the time to completion at a given temperature the program calculates the time for reaction to take place at any other selected temperature based on the use of the Arrhenius equation, (Equation (3.7)). Although the input reaction time is entered in seconds, the output is arranged to be in the most suitable time units for the reaction period calculated.

```
100 INIT
110 PAGE
120 REM 3.2 REACTION TIMES FROM ACTIVATION ENERGY
150 PRINT "ENTER ACTIVATION ENERGY (Q) IN KJ/MOL/K"
160 INPUT Q
170 Q=Q*1000
180 PRINT "ENTER KNOWN TIME IN SECS FOR REACTION AND";
185 PRINT " CORRESPONDING TEMP oC"
190 INPUT S1,T1
200 R=0
210 IF R<>0 THEN 230
220 GO TO 240
230 PAGE
240 PRINT
250 PRINT "ENTER TEMP oC AT WHICH REACTION TIME IS REQUIRED"
260 INPUT T2
270 R=8.314
280 K1=T1+273
290 K2=T2+273
300 S2=EXP(Q/(R*K2))/EXP(Q/(R*K1))*S1
310 IF S2>3600*24*365 THEN 360
320 IF S2>3600*7 THEN 390
330 IF S2>3600 THEN 420
340 IF S2>60 THEN 450
350 GO TO 480
360 S2=S2/(3600*24*365)
370 A$="YEARS"
380 GO TO 490
390 S2=S2/(3600*24)
400 A$="DAYS"
410 GO TO 490
```

```
420 S2=S2/3600
430 A$="HOURS"
440 GO TO 490
450 S2=S2/60
460 A$="MINS"
470 GO TO 490
480 A$="SECS"
490 PRINT
500 PRINT
510 PRINT "TIME FOR REACTION AT ";T2;" oC IS ";S2;" ";A$
520 PRINT "------------------------------------------------------"
530 PRINT
540 PRINT
550 PRINT "ENTER C TO RE-RUN AT ANOTHER TEMPERATURE"
560 INPUT B$
570 IF B$="C" THEN 210
580 END
```

Program notes

(1) All necessary operator input is completed by line 260.
(2) Lines 200–210 control clearing of the VDU for other than an initial run. If a run has taken place R will have been assigned the value of the gas constant in line 270 and will not, therefore, be zero.
(3) Conversion of input temperatures from °C to kelvins takes place in lines 280–290 and the calculation of reaction time is done in line 300.
(4) Lines 360–480 decide the most appropriate time units for print-out and assign the appropriate label to A string.
(5) The output and an option to re-run is completed in lines 490–570. A re-run begins at line 210 and, therefore, does not require the input of activation energy, etc., nor is the program title printed on output of result.

Program 3.3: Calculation of diffusion profiles – Fick's second law

The program calculates and displays graphically a diffusion profile for the ingress of a solute species into a metallic solvent to a depth of 5 mm. Calculation is based on a specific solution to Fick's second law, Equation (3.11). The solution of Equation (3.11) used is for the case of an infinite source on a semi-infinite metal slab

$$\frac{C_s - C_x}{C_x - C_0} = \operatorname{erf}\left(\frac{x}{2\sqrt{Dt}}\right) \tag{3.31}$$

where C_s is the concentration of the solute at the surface, C_0 is the base concentration of the solute in the solvent and C_x is the solute concentration at a distance x into the slab. The value of erf $(x/2\sqrt{Dt})$ is the Gaussian error function presented in Table 3.5. The example used in running the program is the diffusion of carbon into steel at 1000°C and the following values apply: $C_s = 0.93$ wt % C, $C_0 = 0.1$ wt % C and D (1000°C) $= 0.31 \times 10^{-6}$ cm^2/sec.

Table 3.5 Error functions

$x/2\sqrt{Dt}$	$erf(x/2\sqrt{Dt})$
0	0
0.10	0.113
0.20	0.223
0.40	0.428
0.60	0.604
0.80	0.742
1.00	0.843
1.25	0.923
1.50	0.966
2.00	0.995
∞	1.000

```
100 INIT
110 PAGE
120 REM 3.3 CALCULATION OF DIFF. PROFILES-FICK'S 2nd LAW
150 DIM A(10),B(10),C(51),D1(51),E1(51)
160 DATA 0,0.1,0.2,0.4,0.6,0.8,1,1.25,1.5,2
170 READ A
180 DATA 0,0.113,0.223,0.428,0.604,0.742,0.843,0.923,0.966
185 DATA 0.995
190 READ B
200 PRINT "ENTER DIFF. COEFF. cm^2/SEC AT APPROPRIATE TEMP"
210 INPUT D
220 PRINT "ENTER CONCS. IN Wt% FOR SURFACE AND BASE COMPNS"
230 INPUT C1,C0
240 I1=0
250 PRINT "ENTER TIME AT WHICH PROFILE IS REQUIRED IN SECS"
260 INPUT T
270 FOR X=0 TO 0.5 STEP 0.01
280 X1=X/(2*SQR(D*T))
290 GOSUB 1000
300 C2=C1-(C1-C0)*E
310 C(X*100+1)=C2
320 D1(X*100+1)=X
330 E1(X*100+1)=E
340 NEXT X
350 IF I1<>0 THEN 370
360 PAGE
370 I1=I1+1
380 VIEWPORT 0,100,0,80
390 WINDOW 0,0.5,0,1
400 IF I1>1 THEN 420
410 AXIS 0.1,0.1,0,0
420 DRAW D1,C
430 VIEWPORT 0,130,0,100
440 WINDOW 0,130,0,100
450 MOVE 0,100
460 GO TO 250
470 END
1000 REM LINEAR INTERPOLATION FOR ERROR FUNCTION
1010 FOR I=1 TO 10
1020 IF X1>2 THEN 1040
1030 GO TO 1060
1040 E=1
1050 GO TO 1140
1060 IF X1=A(I) THEN 1110
1070 IF X1>A(I) THEN 1130
1080 I=I-1
1090 E=B(I)+(X1-A(I))/(A(I+1)-A(I))*(B(I+1)-B(I))
1100 GO TO 1140
```

```
1110 E=B(I)
1120 GO TO 1140
1130 NEXT I
1140 RETURN
```

Program notes

(1) Lines 160 and 180 contain the error function data from Table 3.5 to be stored in arrays A and B which are dimensioned in line 150 together with storage arrays for the plotting variables D1 and C.

(2) Required input data are completed by line 260. The I1 = 0 in line 240 is used in conjunction with lines 350 and 370 to control screen clearing.

(3) Calculation of concentration of solute with distance (0.1 mm intervals) is contained within the FOR . . . NEXT loop, lines 270–340.

(4) Selection of the correct value of the error function is done within sub-routine 1000, including linear interpolation between stored values where appropriate.

(5) Lines 380–470 control the graphics output.

Program 3.4: Analysis of resistivity data: Johnson–Mehl

This program is based on the ideas expressed in Section 3.5 together with Equations (3.12–3.14). Experimental data derived by measuring changes in electrical resistivity with time using a standard null

Table 3.6

Sample width (cms): 0.460
Sample thickness (cms): 0.060
Solution annealed resistivity (microhm cms): 9.8449
Fully reacted resistivity (microhm cms): 5.3697

Time (min)	Standard voltage (V)	Sample voltage (V)
5	0.001937	0.001231
10	0.001939	0.001209
15	0.001936	0.001173
20	0.001937	0.001132
40	0.001940	0.001047
80	0.001939	0.000972
150	0.001936	0.000921

reading potentiometric technique can be massaged and analysed to provide results which indicate the progress of a reaction and an indication of the mechanism involved via determination of the time exponent. Typical data from a precipitation hardening system are presented in Table 3.6 and are used in the running of the program.

```
100 PAGE
110 INIT
120 REM 3.4 ANALYSIS OF RESISTIVITY DATA - JOHNSON-MEHL
160 PRINT "ENTER NUMBER OF DATA SETS"
170 INPUT Z
180 PRINT " ENTER WIDTH, THICKNESS OF SAMPLE IN cms"
190 INPUT W,T
200 PRINT "ENTER SOLUTION ANNEALED RESIST.,";
205 PRINT " FULLY REACTED RESIST."
210 INPUT S,K
220 L=1.8
230 A=W*T
240 DIM R(Z),C(Z),V1(Z),V2(Z),Y(Z),P(Z),M(Z),X1(Z),Y1(Z)
250 PRINT "ENTER STANDARD VOLTAGE; VOLTS"
260 INPUT V1
270 PRINT "ENTER SAMPLE VOLTAGE; VOLTS"
280 INPUT V2
290 PRINT "ENTER TIMES IN MINUTES"
300 INPUT M
310 FOR H=1 TO Z
320 Q=V2(H)/V1(H)*1000*(A/1.8)
330 R(H)=Q
340 Q1=1.7241/R(H)*100
350 C(H)=Q1
360 IF S=0 THEN 420
370 Q2=(S-R(H))/(S-K)
380 Y(H)=Q2
390 Q3=LGT(1/(1-Y(H)))
400 Q4=LGT(Q3)
410 P(H)=Q4
420 NEXT H
430 PAGE
440 PRINT "DATE...........                    ";
445 PRINT "SPECIMEN NO:........"
450 PRINT
460 PRINT
470 PRINT
480 A$="TIME(MINS)"
490 B$="RESISTIVITY"
500 C$="% I.A.C.S."
510 D$="Y"
520 E$="LOG(LOG1/(1-Y))"
530 IMAGE 2X,10A, 4X,11A,4X,10A,9X,1A,6X,15A
540 PRINT USING 530:A$,B$,C$,D$,E$
550 PRINT
560 FOR J=1 TO Z
570 IMAGE5X,4D,9X,2D.4D,8X,2D.2D,10X
580 IMAGE5X,4D,9X,2D.4D,8X,2D.2D,10X,1D.3D,7X,2D.4D,3X
590 IF S=0 THEN 620
600 PRINT USING 580:M(J),R(J),C(J),Y(J),P(J)
610 GO TO 630
620 PRINT USING 570:M(J),R(J),C(J)
630 NEXT J
640 IF S=0 THEN 750
650 PRINT
660 PRINT
670 PRINT
680 FOR I=1 TO Z
690 X1(I)=LGT(M(I))
700 Y1(I)=P(I)
710 NEXT I
720 GOSUB 1000
730 PRINT "TIME EXPONENT =",M
740 PRINT "Correlation Coefficient=",R
750 END
1000 REM TO PLOT BEST STRAIGHT LINE THROUGH POINTS
1010 DELETE X,N,Y,C,L,M,R
1020 N=Z
```

```
1030 DIM X(N+7),Y(N+7)
1040 FOR I=1 TO Z
1050 X(I)=X1(I)
1060 Y(I)=Y1(I)
1070 NEXT I
1080 E1=0
1090 E2=0
1100 E3=0
1110 E4=0
1120 E5=0
1130 FOR I=1 TO N
1140 E1=E1+X(I)
1150 E2=E2+X(I)*X(I)
1160 E3=E3+Y(I)
1170 E4=E4+Y(I)*Y(I)
1180 E5=E5+X(I)*Y(I)
1190 NEXT I
1200 M=(E5-E1*E3/N)/(E2-E1*E1/N)
1210 C=(E1*E5-E3*E2)/(E1*E1-N*E2)
1220 S=((E2-E1*E1/N)*(E4-E3*E3/N))^0.5
1230 R=(E5-E1*E3/N)/S
1240 K=((E4-E3*E3/N-M*R*S)/(N-2))^0.5
1250 REM SELECT VALUE OF T
1260 IF N-2=1 THEN 1460
1270 IF N-2=2 THEN 1480
1280 IF N-2=3 THEN 1500
1290 IF N-2=4 THEN 1520
1300 IF N-2=5 THEN 1540
1310 IF N-2=6 THEN 1560
1320 IF N-2=7 THEN 1580
1330 IF N-2=8 THEN 1600
1340 IF N-2=9 THEN 1620
1350 IF N-2=10 THEN 1640
1360 IF N-2<13 THEN 1660
1370 IF N-2<16 THEN 1680
1380 IF N-2<21 THEN 1700
1390 IF N-2<25 THEN 1720
1400 IF N-2<31 THEN 1740
1410 IF N-2<41 THEN 1760
1420 IF N-2<61 THEN 1780
1430 IF N-2<121 THEN 1800
1440 T=1.96
1450 GO TO 1810
1460 T=12.71
1470 GO TO 1810
1480 T=4.3
1490 GO TO 1810
1500 T=3.18
1510 GO TO 1810
1520 T=2.78
1530 GO TO 1810
1540 T=2.57
1550 GO TO 1810
1560 T=2.45
1570 GO TO 1810
1580 T=2.36
1590 GO TO 1810
1600 T=2.31
1610 GO TO 1810
1620 T=2.26
1630 GO TO 1810
1640 T=2.23
1650 GO TO 1810
1660 T=2.18
1670 GO TO 1810
1680 T=2.13
1690 GO TO 1810
1700 T=2.09
```

```
1710 GO TO 1810
1720 T=2.06
1730 GO TO 1810
1740 T=2.04
1750 GO TO 1810
1760 T=2.02
1770 GO TO 1810
1780 T=2
1790 GO TO 1810
1800 T=1.98
1810 U=M+K*T*(N/(N*E2-E1*E1))^0.5
1820 L=2*M-U
1830 RETURN
```

Program notes

(1) All required input data and dimensioning of storage arrays are completed by line 300. Values of solution annealed and fully reacted resistivities requested in line 200 provide the start and end points against which reaction progress is measured. If it is only required to convert experimental data to resistivities (microhm cms) and % IACS (international annealed copper scale) and not to have a full analysis, then this may be achieved by entering zeros for solution annealed and fully reacted. This program assumes a standard length of sample, L = 1.8 cm in line 220.

(2) All necessary calculations and conversions to provide the output are completed within the FOR . . . NEXT loop, lines 310–420.

(3) Lines 440–630 provide the tabulated output by utilizing PRINT USING and IMAGE statement.

(4) The statement S = 0 in line 590 produces a simplified output format commensurate with the lack of data at line 210. The conditional statement in line 640 will cause the program to terminate if S = 0.

(5) Lines 670–700 exchange variables needed for full analysis from their current data storage arrays to arrays X1 and Y1 required by sub-routine 1000.

(6) Sub-routine 1000 is a standard linear regression program identical with that used in Program 3.1 (see Program note 8 – Program 3.1).

(7) After sub-routine 1000 a return to line 720 completes the output.

Program 3.5: Determination of hardenability

The main part of the program is based on Equations (3.17–3.21) and Tables 3.2–3.3 contained in Section 3.6. From an input of grain size, carbon content and up to six metallic alloying additions, the program calculates the hardenability. The program is valid for carbon contents up to 0.6% carbon and for grain sizes and metallic alloying additions within the limits prescribed in Tables 3.2 and 3.3. If any of the boundaries are exceeded, an appropriate output is initiated.

In addition to calculation of hardenability the program also calculates and outputs the following:

(a) A_3 — the upper critical temperature,
(b) M_s — the martensitic start temperature,
(c) M_f — the martensitic finish temperature,
(d) B_s — the bainitic start temperature, and
(e) B_f — the bainitic finish temperature.

The empirical formulae used to calculate the above temperatures are not quoted separately but are contained in lines 1490–1590 of the program.

```
100 PAGE
110 INIT
120 REM 3.5 DETERMINATION OF HARDENABILITY
150 PRINT "ENTER GRAIN SIZE No AND CARBON CONTENT IN Wt%"
160 INPUT Z,C
170 IF C=0.25 THEN 190
180 IF C<0.25 AND Z>9 OR (C<0.25 AND Z<6) THEN 1450
190 IF C>0.25 AND Z>8 OR Z<5 THEN 1450
200 IF C=0 THEN 1470
210 Z=Z-5
220 PRINT "ENTER %wt OF Si,Mn,Cr,Mo,Ni,Cu-in order";
225 PRINT "-include zero return"
230 INPUT S,M,G,Y,N,K
240 DIM C1(4,4),C2(4,4)
250 IF C>0.2499 THEN 300
260 DATA 0.0342,0.0337,0.0272,0.0252,2.1774,2.0143,1.9488
270 DATA 1.788,-1.5,-1.333,-1.4048,-1.1905,0,0,0,0
280 READ C1
290 GO TO 350
300 DATA -0.1552,-0.1448,-0.119,-0.1638,3.7559,3.5441,3.2617
310 DATA 3.4224,-4.7143,-4.5003,-4.2499,-4.7499,2.1296
315 DATA 2.0373,2.0369,2.4074
320 RESTORE 300
330 READ C2
340 GO TO 410
350 D1=0
360 FOR I=0 TO 3
370 D0=C1(I+1,Z)*C^I
380 D1=D1+D0
390 NEXT I
400 GO TO 470
410 D1=0
420 Z=Z+1
430 FOR I=0 TO 3
440 D0=C2(I+1,Z)*C^I
450 D1=D1+D0
460 NEXT I
470 F1=0
480 F2=0
490 F3=0
500 F4=0
510 F5=0
520 F6=0
530 IF C>0.25 THEN 790
540 DIM S1(7),M1(7),G1(7),N1(7),Y1(7),Y2(7)
550 DATA 1.002,0.0071,-0.1994,0.3802,-0.1091,0,0,0.994
560 DATA 0.6605,1.9863,-1.2143,0.2868,0,0,1.0568,-0.6407
570 DATA 5.3626,-7.0685,4.1646,-0.7779,0,1.0033,-0.0105
575 DATA 1.1255,-1.3864,0.754,-0.1862,0.0175,0.9908,1.196
580 DATA 1.0489,-0.2348,0,0,0,1.636,-1.139,3.399,0,0,0,0
```

```
590 RESTORE 550
600 READ S1,M1,G1,N1,Y1,Y2
610 FOR I=0 TO 6
620 F=S1(I+1)*(S+1.0E-20)^I
630 F1=F+F1
640 F=M1(I+1)*(M+1.0E-20)^I
650 F2=F+F2
660 F=G1(I+1)*(G+1.0E-20)^I
670 F3=F+F3
680 F=N1(I+1)*(N+1.0E-20)^I
690 F4=F+F4
700 IF N>1 THEN 740
710 F=Y1(I+1)*(Y+1.0E-20)^I
720 F5=F+F5
730 GO TO 770
740 IF Y<0.65 OR Y>1 THEN 710
750 F=Y2(I+1)*(Y+1.0E-20)^I
760 F5=F+F5
770 NEXT I
780 GO TO 1100
790 DIM S2(7),M2(7),M3(7),G2(7),Y3(7),Y4(7),N2(7),K1(7)
800 DATA 0.9949,0.5215,-0.6969,0.6173,-0.1368,0,0,0.9945
810 DATA 0.456,-0.4136,0.6029,0,0,0,-3.56,7.17,-2.67,0.461
820 DATA 0,0,0,0.9802,2.006,-1.9313,3.4874,-2.5915,0.8537
830 DATA -0.1034,0.9761,2.406,-1.3661,0.4996,0,0,0,1.5096
840 DATA -5.457,14.7053,-7.5578,0,0,0,0,0.9834,1.7184,-1.3489
845 DATA 0.305,0.0731,-0.024,0,0,0.9938,1.6343,-1.5615
850 DATA 0.7876,-0.1442,0,0
860 RESTORE 800
870 READ S2,M2,M3,G2,Y3,Y4,N2,K1
880 FOR I=0 TO 6
890 F=S2(I+1)*(S+1.0E-20)^I
900 F1=F+F1
910 IF M>1.1999 THEN 950
920 F=M2(I+1)*(M+1.0E-20)^I
930 F2=F+F2
940 GO TO 970
950 F=M3(I+1)*(M+1.0E-20)^I
960 F2=F+F2
970 F=G2(I+1)*(G+1.0E-20)^I
980 F3=F+F3
990 IF Y>0.6499 THEN 1030
1000 F=Y3(I+1)*(Y+1.0E-20)^I
1010 F5=F+F5
1020 GO TO 1050
1030 F=Y4(I+1)*(Y+1.0E-20)^I
1040 F5=F+F5
1050 F=N2(I+1)*(N+1.0E-20)^I
1060 F4=F+F4
1070 F=K1(I+1)*(K+1.0E-20)^I
1080 F6=F+F6
1090 NEXT I
1100 IF F1=0 THEN 1120
1110 GO TO 1130
1120 F1=1
1130 IF F2=0 THEN 1150
1140 GO TO 1160
1150 F2=1
1160 IF F3=0 THEN 1180
1170 GO TO 1190
1180 F3=1
1190 IF F4=0 THEN 1210
1200 GO TO 1220
1210 F4=1
1220 IF F5=0 THEN 1240
1230 GO TO 1250
1240 F5=1
1250 IF F6=0 THEN 1270
1260 GO TO 1280
1270 F6=1
```

```
1280 D2=D1*F1*F2*F3*F4*F5*F6
1290 D=INT(D2*100)/100
1300 PRINT
1310 PRINT "----------------------------------------------------"
1320 PRINT
1330 PRINT "HARDENABILITY = ";D;" inches -ie ";
1335 PRINT INT(D*25.4);" mm"
1340 PRINT
1350 PRINT "----------------------------------------------------"
1360 IF C>0.25 THEN 1390
1370 IF S>2 OR M>1.4 OR G>1.65 OR Y>1 OR N>3.75 THEN 1410
1380 GO TO 1490
1390 IF C>0.6 OR S>2 OR M>2.5 OR G>2.8 OR Y>1 THEN 1410
1395 IF N>3 OR K>2 THEN 1410
1400 GO TO 1490
1410 PRINT
1420 PRINT "Result is suspect - coefficient(s) are outside"
1430 PRINT " limits for certain element(s)."
1440 GO TO 1490
1450 PRINT "Grain Size No. entered is outside data range"
1460 GO TO 1590
1470 PRINT "Zero Carbon content - unrealistic specification"
1480 IF C=0 THEN 1590
1490 A=910-203*SQR(C)-15.2*N+44.7*S+31.5*Y
1500 V=539-423*C-30.4*M-17.7*N-12.1*G-7.5*Y
1510 B=830-270*C-90*M-37*N-70*G-83*Y
1520 PRINT "Ac3= ";INT(A);" oC"
1530 PRINT
1540 PRINT "Ms = ";INT(V);" oC"
1550 PRINT "Mf = ";INT(V-215);" oC"
1560 PRINT
1570 PRINT "Bs = ";INT(B);" oC"
1580 PRINT "Bf = ";INT(B-220);" oC"
1590 END
```

Program notes

(1) All operator input data entries are completed by line 230.

(2) Line 240 dimensions data storage arrays for carbon coefficients appropriate to the two carbon ranges.

(3) Line 250 is a conditional branch determining which set of carbon data are read, i.e. for low- or medium-carbon steels.

(4) Calculation of D_1^0 (D1) is calculated either in lines 360–380 or lines 430–460, again depending on carbon range.

(5) Lines 470–520 initiate variables to be used in calculating the effect of individual metallic alloying additions.

(6) Line 530 sets up a conditional branch ensuring data appropriate to carbon content is read.

(7) Lines 540–770 dimension storage arrays, contain data and calculate the effect of individual metallic alloy additions for steels of between 0.25 and 0.6 wt % C. Lines 790–1090 do likewise for steels containing less than 0.25 wt % C.

(8) If any of the power series for individual elements are zero they must be reset to one before the final produce (line 1280) is determined. This process is completed in lines 1100–1270.

(9) Checks are made on the validity of input specification against data ranges in lines 1360–1400 and an appropriate warning concerning the result is printed if any element is outside valid data range.

Program 3.6: Corrosion — calculation of cell voltages

The program utilizes the Nernst equation, Equation (3.23), to calculate the half-cell potentials for anode and cathode and hence the total cell voltage by difference, Equation (3.24). A small data base of standard electrode potentials is included which could be readily extended to cover a much bigger range. Apart from the standard electrode potential selected from the data base the program requires input of pure metal and electrode ion activities together with the temperature of each electrode.

```
100 INIT
110 PAGE
120 REM 3.6 CORROSION-CALCULATION OF CELL VOLTAGES
140 DIM N(17)
150 DATA -3.045,-2.925,-2.923,-2.906,-2.866,-2.714,-2.363
160 DATA -1.662,-0.7628,-0.4402,-0.4029,-0.136,-0.126,-0.036
170 DATA 0.337,0.7991,0.854,8.3143,96486
180 READ N,R,F
190 PRINT "Data Base"
200 PRINT "---------"
210 PRINT "Lithium(1)-1+      Potassium(2)-1+      Cesium(3)-1+"
220 PRINT "Barium(4)-2+       Calcium(5)-2+        Sodium(6)-1+"
230 PRINT "Magnesium(7)-2+    Aluminium(8)-3+      Zinc(9)-2+"
240 PRINT "Iron(10)-2+        Cadmium(11)-2+       Tin(12)-2+"
250 PRINT "Lead(13)-2+        Iron(14)-3+          Copper(15)-2+"
260 PRINT "Silver(16)-1+      Mercury(17)-2+"
270 PRINT
280 PRINT "N.B.Enter elements as number given in brackets"
290 PRINT
300 PRINT "ENTER CATHODE METAL AND VALENCY"
310 INPUT N1,V
320 PRINT "ENTER ACTIVITY OF PURE METAL (usually 1)"
330 INPUT A0
340 PRINT "ENTER ACTIVITY OF CATHODE IONS"
350 INPUT A2
360 PRINT "ENTER TEMPERATURE oC"
370 INPUT T
380 T=T+273
390 E1=N(N1)-R*T/(V*F)*LOG(A0/A2)
400 PRINT "ENTER ANODE METAL AND VALENCY"
410 INPUT N1,V
420 PRINT "ENTER ACTIVITY OF PURE METAL (usually 1)"
430 INPUT A0
440 PRINT "ENTER ACTIVITY OF ANODE IONS"
450 INPUT A2
460 PRINT "ENTER TEMPERATURE"
470 INPUT T
480 T=T+273
490 E2=N(N1)-R*T/(V*F)*LOG(A0/A2)
500 E=E1-E2
510 PRINT "-----------------------------------------"
520 PRINT
530 PRINT "CELL VOLTAGE = ";INT(E*1000)/1000;" VOLTS"
540 IF E=>0 THEN 560
550 PRINT "ELECTRODES INCORRECTLY SELECTED"
560 END
```

Program notes

(1) Storage for the data base is dimensioned in line 140. Data on the standard electrode potentials is contained in lines 150–160 and read

as the first data item in line 180 together with values of the gas constant and the Faraday constant.
(2) Lines 210–260 produce a screen display of the metals included in the data base.
(3) Required operator input for the cathode metal is requested and processed in lines 300–390.
(4) The anode metal is similarly dealt with in lines 400–490.
(5) Final determination of cell voltage and output is completed in lines 500–560.

PROBLEMS

(3.1) Modify Program 3.1 to produce a graphics output for $(wt/\text{area})^2$ against time for each temperature and also for the final Arrhenius plot. It would be good practice to write an original routine for accomplishing this, but sub-routine 2000 of Program 5.2 could be used if desired.

(3.2) Using Program 3.1 as a guide, write a program to calculate activation energy utilizing a different determining parameter such as hardness or resistivity.

(3.3) (Program 3.2) The activation energy for recystallization is 120 KJ/Mol/K. If recrystallization is complete in 15 min at a tempera- of 500°C, how long will it take at 520°C?

(3.4) Run Program 3.3 for a series of times to observe the effect. It will be noticed that each time entered overprints the previous times. Modify the program so that the times investigated are listed one beneath the other.

Further modify the program so that each time has a reference number, e.g. 600 s—1, and arrange to have each profile drawn, labelled with its identifying number.

(3.5) Modify Program 3.4 in the following ways:

   (a) Allow the length of sample, L, to be operator entered as a variable.
   (b) Arrange for the program to request date, material identification, etc. as part of the program run and modify the output to suit.

(3.6) Use Program 3.5 to investigate the relative effect of the metallic alloying additions on hardenability.

(3.7) Using steel specifications from the last book listed in the bibliography (or some similar publication) compare hardenabilities calculated by Program 3.5 with the published values. Enter some specifications outside the suggested limits given in Tables 3.2 and 3.3 and observe the effects.

(3.8) Program 3.5 will state when 'coefficient(s) are outside limits for certain elements'. Modify the program to print which specific element(s) is/are outside limits.

(3.9) Using the paper by Deb[4] *et al.*, extend Program 3.5 to include high-carbon steels.

(3.10) Modify Program 3.6 in the following ways:

(a) Increase the data base.

(b) Arrange for the elemental names of the electrodes to be included in the final output. Apply this also to a situation where electrodes were incorrectly selected.

References

(1) Kubaschewski, Evans and Alcock, *Metallurgical Thermo-chemistry*, Pergamon Press, Oxford, (1967).

(2) Johnson, W. A. and Mehl, R. F., *Trans. AIME.*, **135**, 416, (1939).

(3) Burke, *The Kinetics of Phase Transformation in Metals*, Pergamon Press, Oxford, pp. 192 (1965)

(4) Deb, Chaturvedi and Jena, 'Analytical representation of hardenability data for steels', *Metals Tech.*, **9**, (Feb. 1982).

Bibliography

Swalin, R. A., *Thermodynamics of Solids*, John Wiley and Sons, Inc., New York.

Szekely, J. and Thermelis, N. J., *Rate Phenomena in Process Metal-lurgy*, John Wiley and Sons, Inc., New York, (1971).

Uhlig, H. H., *Corrosion and Corrosion Control*, John Wiley and Sons, New York, (1963).

Darken, L. S. and Gurry, R. W., *Physical Chemistry of Metals*, McGraw-Hill Book Co. Inc., (1953).

Burke, J., *The Kinetics of Phase Transformations in Metals*, Pergamon Press, (1965).

Chapter 4

Mechanical properties of polymers

ESSENTIAL THEORY

4.1 Introduction

The mechanical properties of polymers are dependent on the atoms in the mer, the molecular weight and the bonding between molecules. This chapter deals first with the size of polymer molecules, the number of repeat units in their structure and the ways in which molecular weight can be defined and measured. The general mechanical properties covered are the energy stored in elastic deformation and the work done in permanent or plastic deformation. These programs are, of course, valid for all materials that undergo elastic or permanent deformation. Consideration is then given to the stress or strain relaxation in anelastic materials. The use of simple models for the simulation of the modulus for viscoelastic materials provides a good illustration of the value of a simple computer program. Finally, two sections deal with the influence of molecular structure on strength for elastomers and for a typical polymer.

4.2 Degree of polymerization

The molecular weights of polymers are always large and it is often of interest to know how many mers or units are bonded together in a typical polymer molecule. The degree of polymerization is defined as the molecular weight of the polymer divided by the molecular weight of the mer. Polymer molecules typically contain carbon, hydrogen and oxygen atoms but may also contain other elements. Polyvinyl chloride, for instance, has a mer containing two carbon, three hydrogen and one chlorine atom.

Program 4.1 (p. 84) enables the degree of polymerization of a polymer to be determined, knowing only the number of each individual type of atom in the mer. Allowance is made for ten different elements but the list can easily be extended.

4.3 Average molecular weights

Reference was made in the previous section to the molecular weight of a polymer, but most polymers contain molecules with a considerable range of molecular weights rather than with one specific weight. In a situation such as this, the phrase mean molecular weight needs more close definition. This is particularly so since molecular weight normally has to be determined indirectly by some physical property of the polymer such as its viscosity or ability to scatter light.

The simplest way of expressing a mean molecular weight is to take the weight of a polymer sample and divide that by the number of molecules in the sample. This is the 'number average' molecular weight M_n and can be expressed mathematically as

$$M_n = \frac{\text{Weight of sample}}{\text{Total number of molecules}} = \frac{\Sigma W_i}{\Sigma N_i} = \frac{\Sigma N_i M_i}{\Sigma N_i}$$

where the fraction, i, has a weight of W_i and contains N_i molecules whose molecular weight is M_i.

The property of strength is generally considered to relate to the number average molecular weight. Some properties such as viscosity, however, are more influenced by the larger molecules in a sample than by the smaller ones. An alternative definition of 'weight average' molecular weight, M_w, is used in this case and this can be expressed mathematically as

$$M_w = \frac{\Sigma W_i M_i}{\Sigma W_i} = \frac{\Sigma N_i M_i^2}{\Sigma N_i M_i}$$

M_w is always larger than M_n and the ratio M_w/M_n is used as a measure of the spread of molecular weights of the samples.

The assessment of average molecular weight is usually done on the basis of a set of experimental results which can be plotted as a histogram or distribution of weight fraction against molecular weight similar to that shown in Figure 4.1. There is usually a minimum and maximum molecular weight for which no reading is obtained and a series of experimental values with a corresponding molecular weight associated with each, which, if plotted, produce a distribution similar to that shown in Figure 4.1. The molecular weight readings are not necessarily equally spaced and Program 4.2 (p. 85) takes account of that. The experimental points of E, the instrumental reading, against M the molecular weight, are treated as a histogram as shown in Figure 4.1. The blocks are constructed by putting their boundaries at the molecular weight value exactly between two experimentally determined values. The height of the

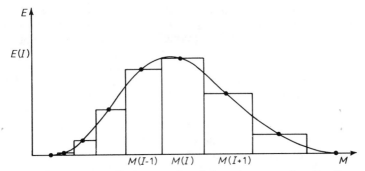

Figure 4.1 Schematic representation of plot of instrumental reading E
against molecular weight M

blocks is that relevant to the particular value of molecular weight
entered. Hence the diagram of the form shown in Figure 4.1 is
achieved. It is assumed, as is normally the case, that the experimental reading, E, is proportional to the weight faction of molecules
present within a given molecular weight range. If this is so, we can
write the formulae for number average and weight average molecular weights in the following forms

$$M_n = \frac{\Sigma E(I) \times \dfrac{M(I+1) - M(I-1)}{2}}{\Sigma \dfrac{E(I)}{M(I)} \times \dfrac{M(I+1) - M(I-1)}{2}}$$

$$M_w = \frac{\Sigma E(I)M(I) \times \dfrac{M(I+1) - M(I-1)}{2}}{\Sigma E(I) \times \dfrac{M(I+1) - M(I-1)}{2}}$$

In each case $\dfrac{M(I+1) - M(I-1)}{2}$ is the width of the block.

Clearly the larger the number of experimental points, the more
accurate the calculation will be. A simpler analysis is possible if all
the blocks are the same width as the width term cancels out, but
instrumental readings do not usually provide these data.

4.4 Elastic strain and elastic energy stored

For a material exhibiting classical elasticity, the elastic strain is
always quite small. However, the elastic energy may be quite high if
the elastic modulus is high, and the elastic energy stored in a reasonable volume of specimen can be quite considerable. For instance,

the elastic energy stored in the hull of a ship can be sufficient to cause a brittle fracture to sever the hull into two halves as occurred in the Liberty ships during World War II. One can also show that the maximum elastic energy that can be stored in a cubic metre of spring steel is sufficient to throw the steel, which weighs 7.83 tonnes, a vertical distance of 14 m or 47 ft. The calculation of elastic strain and energy content is extremely simple but can cause difficulty to students, so its calculation by the computer ensures that one obtains the correct units and decimal point. The elastic strain is simply the applied stress divided by the correct elastic modulus, whilst the elastic energy stored per unit volume is one-half the product of the stress and the elastic strain, which equals one-half of the square of the elastic strain multiplied by the elastic modulus. If the length and cross-sectional area of the specimen is specified, then the actual elastic extension can easily be calculated as the strain multiplied by the initial length and the total elastic energy stored is simply the elastic energy per unit volume multiplied by the volume of the specimen. These calculations are all done in succeeding lines in Program 4.3 on p. 87.

4.5 Work done in deformation

The work done on a specimen during elastic deformation is equal to the elastic energy stored (see Section 4.4). However, once plastic deformation starts, energy is used up as mechanical work done on the specimen, most of which is not recoverable. The total work done in fracturing a specimen is a measure of the toughness of the material. The work done per unit volume W can be expressed by the formula

$$W = \int_0^{\epsilon_f} \sigma \, d\epsilon$$

where σ = stress, ϵ = strain, and ϵ_f = strain at fracture. Clearly W is equal to the area under the stress–strain curve. This can easily be evaluated by numerical integration and a simple program (Program 4.4, p. 87) is given which assumes that the initial values of stress and strain are zero.

4.6 Stress or strain relaxation

Anelasticity is the term used to describe materials that exhibit time dependent elastic properties. That is to say the deformation is dependent only on the stress but does not occur the instant the stress is applied. Equally, when the stress is removed, the strain decays to zero but over a finite period of time. A wide variety of materials exhibit time dependent elasticity over widely varying time spans. Elastomers exhibit large time delays, whereas metals exhibit very short time delays and the class of materials we call viscoelastic materials exhibit properties in between these two extremes. If the growth or decay of strain at constant stress is studied in such a material, it is found to obey an exponential law of the type

$$\epsilon = \epsilon_0 \exp\left(-\frac{t}{\lambda}\right)$$

where ϵ = strain at time t, ϵ_0 = initial strain, and λ = relaxation time. Clearly, if values of strain are known at two particular times, then the relaxation time can be calculated. Alternatively, if the relaxation time is known and strain at a particular time, then other values of strain at different times can be calculated using this simple formula. Program 4.5 (p. 88) enables this to be done.

A similar calculation can be done governing the relaxation of stress. If an engineering component is put under stress and its configuration is fixed, as in the case of, for example, a nut and bolt that are tightened, and if the material exhibits anelasticity, the stress locked into the component will decay with time in accordance with the formula above, with stress replacing strain. Hence one may use exactly the same formulation to calculate the relaxed stress after a given period knowing what the relaxation time is.

4.7 Viscoelastic modulus

A material is said to be viscoelastic if it exhibits some of the deformation characteristics of a viscous material and some of an elastic material. Two simple models have been proposed which, if they are applied in the right way, enable the characteristics of real materials to be simulated. The elements of a viscoelastic material are

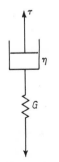

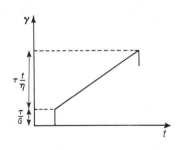

Figure 4.2 Maxwell model of viscoelastic liquid

Figure 4.3 Displacement γ versus time t curve for Maxwell model

considered to be a perfect spring and a perfect dashpot, which allows a piston to pull through it while a stress is applied but stays stationary when the stress is removed. Maxwell combined these two elements in series as a very simple representation of a viscoelastic liquid. This is shown in Figure 4.2 and its displacement versus time curve is shown in Figure 4.3. It is conventional to refer to the stress applied as τ and the displacement as γ

For the spring $\gamma = \tau/G$

For the dashpot $\gamma = t \times \tau/\eta$

In this case the two displacements are additive.

The viscoelastic modulus is, like the elastic modulus, equal to the stress divided by the strain. The difference in the viscoelastic case is that the value of strain varies significantly with time. In this particular case the viscoelastic modulus M is given by the formula

$$M_{ve} = \frac{\tau}{\gamma} = \frac{\tau}{\dfrac{\tau}{G} + \tau\dfrac{t}{\eta}} = \frac{G}{1 + t\dfrac{G}{\eta}}$$

At low values of time, the viscoelastic modulus is equal to G and at high values of time, viscoelastic modulus is equal to zero. The rapid reduction in modulus occurs when $t \times G/\eta = 1$.

It is well known that not all viscoelastic materials behave like a simple liquid in that their modulus at long times is not zero. Many exhibit characteristics of a solid; in other words, their final value of modulus at long times is less than that at short times but not zero. To simulate the properties of such a simple viscoelastic solid the Voigt model is used where the dashpot and spring are put in parallel and must both deform together. This is illustrated in Figure 4.4 and the displacement versus time curve in Figure 4.5. Initially deformation

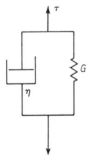

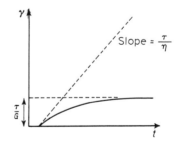

Figure 4.4 Voigt model of viscoelastic solid

Figure 4.5 Displacement γ versus time t curve for Voigt model

is controlled by the dashpot and the displacement versus time starts along a straight line of slope τ divided by η. However, the spring cannot deform indefinitely and it takes over the constraint on the displacement as it is not able to deform to an extent greater than τ/G however long a time is allowed. The displacement γ is given by the formula

$$\gamma = \frac{\tau}{G}\left(1 - \exp\left(-t\frac{G}{\eta}\right)\right)$$

The viscoelastic modulus M_{ve} is given by

$$M_{ve} = \frac{G}{1 - \exp\left(-t\frac{G}{\eta}\right)}$$

At short times the exponential term is close to one, hence the value of modulus is very high. At long times the value of the exponential term becomes zero and the limiting modulus is then equal to G. The transition from a very high modulus to the constant modulus occurs when $t \times G/\eta = 1$. It will be clear that neither of these extremely simple models is able to replicate the performance of real materials in any convincing way. In order to do this the material must be considered as being composed of a series of the units described above so that a real viscoelastic liquid will have a number of Maxwell units connected in parallel, each of which has a different time constant and which, overall, give a much better representation of the way in which a given real material behaves. Equally to replicate a real viscoelastic solid it is possible to combine a number of Voigt units in series with each other, again with different time constants, so that their overall behaviour replicates that of a real viscoelastic solid. A relatively simple computer program enables us to simulate the performance of a number of solid or liquid units and to plot the variation of viscoelastic modulus with time for such a combination. Needless to say, this process is an extremely laborious one to do by hand so here the computer is extremely useful.

4.8 Elastomer stress–strain curve

The stress–strain curve of an elastomer depends on a number of characteristics of the polymer. In particular the density and the number of cross links is important as is the temperature of deformation. A simple formula is available which relates these three parameters to the stress–strain curve and is of the form given below

$$\text{Stress} = C\frac{\rho T}{M_c}\left(\frac{L^2}{L_0^2} - \frac{L_0}{L}\right)$$

where ρ = density, T = absolute temperature, M_c = molecular weight between cross links, L = length, L_0 = initial length, and C = constant.

4.9 Molecular weight and strength of polystyrene

It is widely recognized that the molecular weight of a polymer influences its physical properties. One way of measuring molecular weight is to measure a physical property which changes with molecular weight. The influence of molecular weight on strength is not entirely clear and numerical data are difficult to come by. McCormick et al.[1] studied the effect of molecular weight distribution on the physical properties of polystyrene and it is some of their data in an abbreviated form that are used for this section.

Although it is generally considered that the mechanical properties of polymers are dependent on the number average molecular weight, they found that the weight average molecular weight gave a better correlation with tensile impact strength. A formula of the form

$$\sigma = a - b/M$$

where a and b are constants and M = molecular weight, is fitted to the data and used in Program 4.8. They also found that the tensile strength and elongation were dependent on a molecular weight between the number average and weight average value and these data are considered in the problems on p. 96.

PROGRAMS

Program 4.1: Degree of polymerization

```
100 REM 4.1 DEGREE OF POLYMERISATION
110 PAGE
120 PRINT "ENTER MEAN MOLECULAR WEIGHT g/mol ";
130 INPUT W
140 M=0
150 PRINT "ENTER CHEMICAL SYMBOL OR Z ";
160 INPUT A$
170 IF A$="Z" THEN 230
180 PRINT "ENTER NUMBER OF ATOMS ";
190 INPUT N
200 GOSUB 500
210 M=M+B*N
220 GO TO 150
230 PRINT
240 PRINT "DEGREE OF POLYMERISATION=";INT(W/M)
250 PRINT
260 PRINT "PRESS RETURN TO CONTINUE"
270 INPUT Z$
280 GO TO 100
290 END
500 REM SUBROUTINE FOR ATOMIC WEIGHTS
510 IF A$="H" THEN 630
```

```
520 IF A$="C" THEN 650
530 IF A$="N" THEN 670
540 IF A$="O" THEN 690
550 IF A$="F" THEN 710
560 IF A$="SI" THEN 730
570 IF A$="P" THEN 750
580 IF A$="S" THEN 770
590 IF A$="CL" THEN 790
600 IF A$="BR" THEN 810
610 PRINT "ELEMENT NOT FOUND "
620 GO TO 150
630 B=1.008
640 RETURN
650 B=12.01
660 RETURN
670 B=14.01
680 RETURN
690 B=16
700 RETURN
710 B=19
720 RETURN
730 B=28.09
740 RETURN
750 B=30.97
760 RETURN
770 B=32.06
780 RETURN
790 B=35.45
800 RETURN
810 B=79.91
820 RETURN
```

Program notes

(1) The molecular weight of the polymer is first entered at line 120, after which the chemical symbol of the first element is entered at line 150 and the number of atoms of that element at line 180.

(2) The sub-routine at line 500 searches the list of ten elements and assigns an atomic weight B.

(3) If the element is not present in the list this is registered at line 610 and the program resumes at line 150.

(4) If the symbol, Z, is entered at line 150 the control moves to line 230 and the degree of polymerization is calculated and printed at line 240.

(5) The degree of polymerization is calculated as an integer value, since decimal places clearly have no significance in such large numbers. As with some other programs in this chapter, the computing aspect is trivial, but the ease of access to an interactive result from input data does make it a useful ancillary in a laboratory.

Program 4.2: Weight and number average molecular weights

```
100 REM 4.2 WEIGHT AND NUMBER AVERAGE MOLECULAR WEIGHTS
105 PAGE
110 PRINT "A HISTOGRAM OF EXPERIMENTAL RESULTS VS "
120 PRINT "MOLECULAR WEIGHT DATA IS REQUIRED"
130 PRINT "Enter lowest and highest molecular weights ";
```

```
140 INPUT A,B
150 PRINT "Enter number of readings ";
160 INPUT N
170 DIM E(N+2),M(N+2)
180 M(1)=A
190 M(N+2)=B
200 S=0
210 FOR I=1 TO N
220 PRINT "ENTER E(";I+1;")   MOL WT(";I+1;")";
230 INPUT E(I+1),M(I+1)
240 NEXT I
250 FOR I=1 TO N
260 S=S+E(I+1)*(M(I+2)-M(I))/2
270 NEXT I
280 M1=0
290 M2=0
300 FOR I=1 TO N
310 M1=M1+E(I+1)*(M(I+2)-M(I))/2*M(I+1)/S
320 M2=M2+E(I+1)*(M(I+2)-M(I))/2/M(I+1)/S
330 NEXT I
340 PRINT "Weight average molecular weight ";M1
350 PRINT "Number average molecular weight ";1/M2
360 PRINT "RATIO                          ";M1*M2
370 END
```

Program notes

(1) The lowest and highest molecular weights for which no experimental reading is recorded are entered at line 140 after which the number of experimental readings between those two values is entered at line 160.

(2) The array of values of E and M is then set up at line 170, and the first and last value of the array M are assigned in lines 180 and 190.

(3) Lines 200–230 enable the series of experimental values versus molecular weight to be entered.

(4) Lines 240–270 allow the variable S, which is the area beneath the curve, to be calculated. This is the numerator of the number average molecular weight expression and the denominator of the weight average molecular weight.

(5) The variable M1, which is the weight average molecular weight, is summed in line 310 for all the elements of the array in accordance with the formula above.

(6) The variable M2 which is the inverse of the number average molecular weight is summed at line 320, again in accordance with the formula given above.

(7) Finally, the weight and number average molecular weights are printed and their ratio, which indicates the spread of the molecular sizes, is printed at line 360. The program is designed for unequally spaced data but it is equally suitable if the spacing of the data is equal, but as this case is not the general one, the simpler formulation has not been adopted.

Program 4.3: Elastic strain and energy

```
1100 REM 4.3 ELASTIC STRAIN & ENERGY
105 PAGE
110 PRINT "Enter elastic modulus N/m^2 ";
120 INPUT M
130 PRINT "Enter stress N/m^2 ";
140 INPUT S
150 PRINT "Elastic strain=";S/M
160 PRINT
170 PRINT "Elastic energy/unit volume=";S^2/M/2;" J/m^3"
180 PRINT
190 PRINT "Enter length,cross section in mm ";
200 INPUT L,A
210 PRINT
220 PRINT "Elastic extension=";L*S/M;"mm"
230 PRINT
240 PRINT "Total elastic energy=";S^2/M/2*L*A/1.0E+9;"Joules"
250 PRINT
260 GO TO 110
270 END
```

Program 4.4: Work done in deformation

```
100 REM 4.4 WORK DONE IN DEFORMATION
105 PAGE
110 PRINT "This program calculates the work done during"
120 PRINT "deformation. Stress units are N/m^2"
130 PRINT
150 PRINT "Enter number of readings apart from 0,0 ";
160 INPUT N
170 DIM E(N+1),M(N+1)
180 M(1)=0
190 E(1)=0
200 S=0
210 FOR I=1 TO N
220 PRINT "ENTER STRESS(";I;"), STRAIN(";I;")";
230 INPUT E(I+1),M(I+1)
240 NEXT I
245 PRINT
250 FOR I=1 TO N-1
260 S=S+E(I+1)*(M(I+2)-M(I))/2
270 NEXT I
280 S=S+E(N+1)*(M(N+1)-M(N))/2
290 PRINT "WORK DONE=";S;"J/m^3"
300 END
```

Program notes

(1) The program assumes that the first stress and strain values are both zero. The number of additional points is entered at line 160 and their values at line 230.

(2) S is the area under the curve and for the first N-1 points blocks are set up whose boundaries are midway between the values of strain entered.

(3) The area of these blocks is summed at line 260.

(4) The final block has an upper boundary at the final value of strain entered and the area of this block is added at line 280.

(5) Finally the work done per unit volume is printed.

Program 4.5: Anelastic relaxation time

```
100 REM 4.5 ANELASTIC RELAXATION TIME
110 PAGE
120 PRINT "Calculate or apply relaxation time? (C or A)"
130 INPUT A$
140 IF A$="C" THEN 280
150 IF A$="A" THEN 170
160 GO TO 120
170 PRINT "Enter initial stress or strain ";
180 INPUT S
190 PRINT "Enter relaxation time sec. ";
200 INPUT L
210 PRINT
220 J=INT(LGT(L))
230 FOR N=-2 TO 2
240 PRINT "Value after ";10^(J+N);"sec=";S/EXP(10^(J+N)/L)
250 NEXT N
260 PRINT
270 GO TO 120
280 PRINT "Enter initial stress or strain ";
290 INPUT S1
300 PRINT "Enter final value ";
310 INPUT S2
320 PRINT "Enter time in any units ";
330 INPUT T
340 PRINT "Relaxation time=";T/LOG(S1/S2);"Same units"
350 PRINT
360 GO TO 120
370 END
```

Program notes

(1) The program allows a calculation of relaxation time or its application at line 120.

(2) If application is chosen then the value of the initial stress or strain and the relaxation time are entered at line 180 and 200.

(3) Line 220 selects a value of J that is equal to the power of 10 of the relaxation time in seconds. Thus a relaxation time of 20 seconds will give J = 1, whereas a relaxation time of 9 seconds will give J = 0.

(4) Lines 230–250 print a series of 5 times centred about 10^J and the equivalent stress or strain that applies at those times. Clearly, a wider range of times or a more closely spaced range of times could be easily incorporated in these lines.

(5) If, on running the program, it is required to calculate the relaxation time, the program moves to line 280 when the initial stress or strain and its final value are entered at lines 290 and 310 and the time at which the final value is recorded is entered at line 330.

(6) The simple calculation at line 340 then produces a value of the relaxation time in the same units as the time entered. As in some of the other cases this is a fairly trite calculation but, nevertheless, a convenient one to have at one's fingertips in an interactive set of programs.

Program 4.6: Viscoelastic modulus

```
100 REM 4.6 VISCOELASTIC MODULUS
110 PAGE
120 PRINT "SOLID OR LIQUID ? (S OR L) ";
130 INPUT A$
140 IF A$="L" OR A$="S" THEN 160
150 GO TO 120
160 IF A$="L" THEN 190
170 A=1
180 GO TO 200
190 A=0
200 PAGE
210 PRINT "ENTER NUMBER OF VISCOELASTIC UNITS ";
220 INPUT N
230 IF N<10 THEN 260
240 PRINT "MAX NO IS 9 "
250 GO TO 210
260 DIM M(N),G(N),E(N)
270 FOR I=1 TO N
280 PRINT "ENTER G(";I;"),E(";I;") ";
290 INPUT G(I),E(I)
300 NEXT I
310 FOR J=0 TO 8
320 T=10^J
330 K=0
340 FOR I=1 TO N
350 IF A=1 THEN 420
360 REM LIQUID
370 M(I)=1/G(I)+T/E(I)
380 K=K+1/M(I)
390 NEXT I
400 GO TO 500
410 REM SOLID
420 IF T*G(I)/E(I)<710 THEN 450
430 P=0
440 GO TO 460
450 P=EXP(-T*G(I)/E(I))
460 M(I)=(1-P)/G(I)
470 K=K+M(I)
480 NEXT I
490 K=1/K
500 PRINT
510 PRINT T,K
520 NEXT J
530 PRINT
540 GO TO 120
550 END
```

Program notes

(1) The first few lines assign a value of one to the variable A if the solid model is chosen and zero to A if the liquid model is chosen.

(2) At line 220 the number of units to be treated is entered. It is suggested that this should not exceed 9 but there is no reason why a number larger than 9 should not be used if the operator has the patience to enter the data.

(3) Array variables G for the spring constants and E for the dashpot constants are dimensioned at line 260 together with M which is the inverse of the modulus of the particular element of the material.

(4) Values of G and E for each of the elements are entered at line 290.

(5) Values of time from one second to 10 seconds, which is just over 3 years, are assigned in lines 310 and 320, then at line 340 for each of the elements in the material the inverse of the modulus is calculated.

(6) For the case of the liquid, lines 360–400 calculate the value of the inverse modulus for each of the elements and then sum all the moduli to give K which is the modulus of the assembly of elements. For a solid the introduction of the exponential term makes the calculation a little more complex.

(7) Lines 420–440 are simply there to prevent an overflow on the calculation of the exponential. If the number within the exponential brackets is too large, an error signal is obtained. To overcome this for very large values of the exponential index the value of the variable P is put equal to zero. Again, M(I) is the inverse of the modulus of the element of the material that is being calculated and initially the variable K at line 470 is the inverse modulus of the assembly.

(8) This is inverted at line 490 to give the modulus of the assembly which is then printed at line 510. Thus the print-out gives a value of the viscoelastic modulus for the material chosen with the parameters entered over a range of 10^5 in time. It can be shown mathematically that any combination of Maxwell units in parallel can be matched as far as viscoelastic properties are concerned by a particular set of Voigt units in series. This can be seen in the very simple case of the single Maxwell unit shown in Figure 4.6 and the

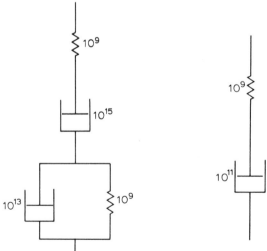

Figure 4.6 Maxwell viscoelastic liquid unit

Figure 4.7 Voigt viscoelastic solid units with combined modulus the same as that of the Maxwell model of *Figure 4.6*

series of two Voigt units shown in Figure 4.7 which, over the span of time covered by the program, give results that are essentially identical. The reader may wish to match similar sets of alternative definitions of viscoelastic solids and liquids to verify this further.

Program 4.7: Elastomer stress–strain

```
100 REM 4.7 ELASTOMER STRESS STRAIN
110 PAGE
120 PRINT "ENTER DENSITY,TEMP C,MOL WT BETWEEN CROSS LINKS"
130 PRINT "DEFAULT VALUES 1.3,20,600 ";
140 INPUT A$,B$,C$
150 IF A$="" THEN 180
160 X=VAL(A$)
170 GO TO 190
180 X=1.3
190 IF B$="" THEN 220
200 Y=VAL(B$)
210 GO TO 230
220 Y=20
230 IF C$="" THEN 260
240 Z=VAL(C$)
250 GO TO 270
260 Z=600
270 D=X*(Y+273)/Z
300 FOR L=1 TO 197 STEP 7
310 PRINT L;"%",((1+L/100)^2-1/(1+L/100))*D*5
320 NEXT L
325 PRINT "Stress units MN/m^2"
330 END
```

Program notes

(1) The required values of density, temperature and molecular weight between cross links can be input at line 140. However default values are built into the program so that a relatively easy comparison can be made with sensible figures.

(2) Lines 150–260 either adopt the default values for these parameters or the input values.

(3) Line 270 calculates the multiplying factor and lines 300–320 tabulate the strain and stress for a particular set of parameters. The output could equally well be a graphical one, but it was felt that a tabulated set of numbers would be the simplest way to illustrate the general nature of the program.

(4) In line 300 the step size allows the number of readings in the table to be varied while leaving the total strain range from 1 to 200%.

(5) In line 310 the numerical multiplication factor of 5 is the constant C and results in the values being in MN/m^2 as is stated at the end of the program.

The reader may feel that a graphical output is much more useful, in which case the program can easily be modified to fill an array of values of strain and stress and to plot those on a graph.

Program 4.8: Molecular weight and tensile impact strength

```
100 REM 4.8 MOLECULAR WEIGHT AND TENSILE IMPACT STRENGTH
110 PAGE
120 PRINT "TENSILE IMPACT STRENGTH OF POLYSTYRENE"
130 PRINT
140 PRINT "Enter weight average molecular weight ";
150 INPUT M
160 IF M<88000 THEN 200
170 PRINT "Tensile impact strength ";5.214-457300/M;" MJ/m^3"
180 PRINT
190 GO TO 140
200 PRINT "NO STRENGTH"
210 GO TO 140
220 END
```

Program notes

(1) The program is extremely simple. After the molecular weight has been entered, if it is less than 88 000, the program moves to line 200 and prints 'no strength'.

(2) If the molecular weight is greater than this value then the calculation of strength is done at line 170 and the result printed at line 180.

As with some of the other programs in this chapter this is an extremely simple one, but nevertheless is useful to have available and to use in an interactive way.

PROBLEMS

(4.1) (Program 4.1) A shorter program can be written which simply asks for the number of carbon, hydrogen, oxygen, etc. atoms and performs a simple calculation on them. For five elements this need be only 15 lines long, but a few more lines are needed to improve the look of the output. The reader may wish to write such a simplified program, but it should be noted that it does not use the logic facilities of the computer as the printed program does.

(4.2) (Program 4.1) As an alternative to storing the atomic weights of specified elements, the mer weights of specified polymers could be stored. The mer weights of a number of common polymers are listed below in Table 4.1.

Table 4.1

Mer	Mer weight
Ethylene	28.052
Propylene	42.078
Acrylonitrile	53.064
Butadiene	54.088
Vinylchloride	62.494
Vinylacetate	86.088
Styrene	99.104

A program could be written in the same form as Program 4.1 but allowing the entry of the name of the mer. An additional element to the program that would print the list of available mers would also be useful.

(4.3) There is another form of average molecular weight which is valid for molecular weight determinations by sedimentation or centrifugal separation, and that is given by the formula below

$$
M_2 = \frac{\Sigma E(I)M(I)^2 \times \dfrac{M(I+1) - M(I-1)}{2}}{\Sigma E(I)M(I) \times \dfrac{M(I+1) - M(I-1)}{2}}
$$

The reader should modify Program 4.2 to include this expression which only requires three further lines.

(4.4) A slightly shorter and simpler version of Program 4.2 could be written if the molecular weight data were equally spaced. The reader should check how much saving in program space is possible by imposing this fairly severe restriction on the input data.

(4.5) As a guide to the user it is possible to introduce into Program 4.3 some comments which indicate the validity of the data that are entered. For instance, if the elastic modulus is between, say, 5×10^{10} N/m^2 and 2.5×10^{11} N/m^2, that would be typical of engineering alloys. Only ceramics have values above 2.5×10^{11} N/m^2 and values between 2×10^8 N/m^2 and 7×10^9 N/m^2 are typical of polymers. Values between 5×10^6 N/m^2 and 3×10^7 N/m^2 are typical of elastomers and comments to this effect could be incorporated in the program. Similarly the value of strain that is calculated could generate a comment.

An elastic strain greater than 0.008 would be very unlikely in a metal and a value greater than 0.0007 would be very unlikely in a ceramic. Polymers could give values as high as 0.03 and elastomers even up to perhaps 2.

The reader should introduce these criteria into the program so that the print out has the following form:

```
Enter elastic modulus N/m^2
 7.0E+10
TYPICAL OF ENGINEERING ALLOY
Enter stress N/m^2
 7.0E+8
Elastic strain=0.01
TOO HIGH FOR A METAL
Enter stress N/m^2
 4.0E+8
Elastic strain=0.00571428571429

Elastic energy/unit volume=1142857.14286 J/m^3
```

```
Enter length,cross section in mm
 100 20

ELAstic extension=0.571428571429mm

Total elastic energy=2.28571428571Joules
```

The program should also be modified so that the energy stored is only calculated if consistent data are entered.

(4.6) A very worthwhile addition to Program 4.4 would be a plot of the stress–strain curve from the starting point (0,0). The reader should add this as a facility to the program.

In the next chapter, Program 5.2 deals with the derivation of engineering and true stresses and strains from force, extension data. data. The present program could also be incorporated into Program 5.2 to give the work done.

(4.7) (Program 4.5) If the material is not simple but has two relaxation mechanisms giving two relaxation times, the formula quoted in Section 4.6 above becomes

$$\epsilon = \epsilon_0 \left\{ f \exp\left(-\frac{t}{\lambda_1}\right) + (1-f) \exp\left(-\frac{t}{\lambda_2}\right) \right\}$$

where f is a numerical factor <1 and λ_1 and λ_2 are the relaxation times. Modify Program 4.5 to allow for the application of two relaxation times and a choice of value of f.

(4.8) Consider how many values of stress and time would be required in order to determine the values of λ_1, λ_2 and f. Modify the initial Program 4.5 to allow for this.

(4.9) (Program 4.6) Try to simulate the properties of propathene at 60°C, whose tensile modulus is found to be

426 MN/m^2 at 100 s
280 MN/m^2 at 10^5 s
200 MN/m^2 at 10^8 s

If a viscoelastic liquid is chosen made of five elements whose values of G/η are 10^{-1}, 10^{-3}, 10^{-5}, 10^{-7} and 10^{-9} we have

$$M = M_1 + M_2 + M_3 + M_4 + M_5$$

where M = overall modulus and M_1 = modulus of element 1, etc. Substituting for the times and modulic three equations result that

$$426 = \frac{G_1}{11} + \frac{G_2}{1.1} + G_3 + G_4 + G_5 \tag{4.1}$$

$$280 = \frac{G_3}{2} + G_4 + G_5 \tag{4.2}$$

$$200 = \frac{G_4}{11} + \frac{G_5}{1.1} \tag{4.3}$$

Equation (4.3) allows for values of G_5 from 0 to 220 if G_4 has values between 2200 and 0. However, in order for G_3 to have a positive value G_4 cannot be too large. Values of 215, 55 and 20 for G_5, G_4 and G_3 respectively satisfy Equations (4.2) and (4.3), and Equation (4.1) is then satisfied by values of 902 and 60 for G_1 and G_2 respectively.

If the program is used to calculate the modulus for a liquid whose elements are

$G_1 = 902 \times 10^6 \, N/m^2$	$\eta_1 = 9.02 \times 10^9 \, Ns/m^2$
$G_2 = 60 \times 10^6 \, N/m^2$	$\eta_2 = 6.0 \times 10^{10} \, Ns/m^2$
$G_3 = 20 \times 10^6 \, N/m^2$	$\eta_3 = 2.0 \times 10^{12} \, Ns/m^2$
$G_4 = 55 \times 10^6 \, N/m^2$	$\eta_4 = 5.5 \times 10^{14} \, Ns/m^2$
$G_5 = 215 \times 10^6 \, N/m^2$	$\eta_5 = 2.15 \times 10^{17} \, Ns/m^2$

the values are found to be very close to those specified.

As an alternative simulate the same set of properties with a five element viscoelastic solid. In this case

$$\frac{1}{M} = \frac{1}{M_1} + \frac{1}{M_2} + \frac{1}{M_3} + \frac{1}{M_4} + \frac{1}{M_5}$$

but a similar procedure can be followed to produce a solution.
(4.10) Show how Program 4.6 can be used to determine the modulus of two elements assembled in the way shown in Figure 4.8 by considering it as a three-element solid.

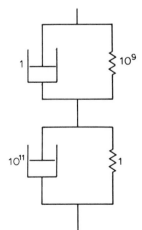

Figure 4.8 Combined Maxwell and Voigt models for Problem 4.10

(4.11) It is much easier to visualize the effects of time on modulus from a graphical representation. Modify Program 4.6 so that it produces a plot of M v. $\log t$ for times from 1 s to 10^8 s.

(4.12) Modify Program 4.7 to calculate the work done in deformation

(1) by adopting the approach described in Program 4.4, i.e. numerical integration and
(2) by integrating the expression in Section 4.8 and adding this to the program.

It is interesting to compare the accuracy of the numerical integration with the analytical solution.

(4.13) As with many of the other programs a graphical output is useful here. Modify Program (4.7) to plot the stress–strain curve.

(4.14) McCormick *et al.* found a similar relationship between tensile strength and a molecular weight between the number average and weight average value. If we define M_s as the mean of M_w and M_n their relationship becomes

$$\text{Tensile strength} = 76.17 - \frac{5.006 \times 10^6}{M_s} \text{MN/m}^2$$

Write a program in the same form as Program 4.8 enabling the tensile strength of polystyrene to be calculated from M_s its mean molecular weight.

Reference

(1) McCormick, H. W., Brewer, F. M. and Kin, L. J., *Polymer Sci.*, **39**, 87–100, (1959).

Bibliography

Van Vlack, L. H., *Materials Science for Engineers*, Addison Wesley, (1982).
Billmeyer, F. W. *Textbook of Polymer Science*, Wiley, (1971).

Chapter 5

Deformation and strength of crystalline materials

ESSENTIAL THEORY

5.1 Introduction

It has long been realized that the deformation and strength of crystalline materials is related to the detailed arrangement of atoms within their regular structures and to the presence of defects, be these of point, line or planar nature, or indeed three-dimensional defects such as cracks. An apparently simple change in the stacking sequence of close-packed layers of atoms as experienced between face-centred-cubic (fcc) and hexagonal-close-packed (hcp), which are ABCABC . . . and ABAB . . . respectively, can make the difference between a mechanically isotropic material and a highly anisotropic one. Small additions of alloying elements to pure metals may affect the number and type defects and hence greatly modify mechanical behaviour. For instance, adding zinc to pure copper, within the primary solid solubility limit, lowers the stacking fault energy, which increases the separation of the partial dislocations, reduces the incidence of cross-slip and, therefore, increases the strain hardening range of the material. In general terms plastic deformation takes place by the sliding, over each other, of planes of highest reticular density (most widely spaced planes) in the most closely packed directions (slip). Thus, any crystal structure may be analysed to discover the likely number of operating slip systems.

Some of the terms used in the introduction to this chapter have been explained more fully in Chapter 2 to which reference should be made if necessary. Deformation and strength incorporate many phenomena and mechanisms. Only a few selected topics have been included, essentially to aid the interpretation and implementation of the programs and to help in solving some of the problems.

5.2 Theoretical strength

Assuming slip to take place by the sliding of one plane of atoms over another, it is possible to make a reasonable estimate of the shear

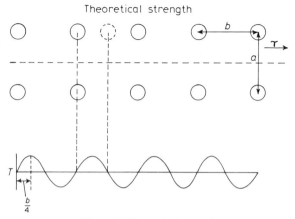

Figure 5.1 Theoretical strength

stress necessary to induce movement in a perfect lattice. Referring to Figure 5.1 and realizing that as the shear stress is increased, the repulsive forces between the atoms will fall much more quickly than will the forces of attraction, then for a first approximation the relationship between shear stress and displacement may be defined by a sine function,

$$\tau = \tau_m \sin \frac{2\pi x}{a} \qquad (5.1)$$

where τ is the applied shear stress, τ_m is the amplitude of the sine wave (theoretical shear strength) and a is the period (distance between atoms in a plane). If only small displacements are involved Hooke's law applies

$$\tau = G\lambda = G\frac{x}{b} \qquad (5.2)$$

where G is the shear modulus and γ the shear strain.

For small values of x/a (Equation (5.1)) sin $(f) \simeq f$. Also since $a \simeq b$ for most metals combining and rearranging Equations (5.1) and (5.2) gives

$$\tau_m = \frac{G}{2\pi} \qquad (5.3)$$

Since the shear modulus range for metals is $10^7 - 10^8\,\text{Nmm}^{-2}$ Equation (5.3) predicts theoretical shear strengths of $10^6 - 10^7\,\text{Nmm}^{-2}$. Actual strengths observed are in the range $10^3 - 10^5\,\text{Nmm}^{-2}$. Thus it must be concluded that slip involves more than the bodily shearing of planes.

A calculation shows that the stress required to move a single dislocation through an otherwise perfect lattice (the Peierls–Nabarro stress) is very much less than the real shear strength of the weakest pure metal. The real shear strength of metals is the shear stress required to move dislocations past barriers, such as solute atoms, other dislocations, second phase particles and grain boundaries. For further details of basic dislocation theory, the reader is referred to the bibliography at the end of this chapter.

5.3 Deformation of single crystals – critical resolved shear stress

The critical resolved shear stress is the single crystal equivalent of yield or flow stress in polycrystalline aggregates. The extent to which slip will take place in a single crystal is dependent on the value of the applied force, the type of crystal structure and the orientation of the most favourable slip direction to the applied force. Slip will commence when the shearing stress on the slip plane reaches a critical value — the critical resolved shear stress. When tensile tests are conducted on single crystals of the same material in different orientations a variety of values for flow stress can result. These may be rationalized by calculating the critical resolved shear stress and was first realized by Schmid[1].

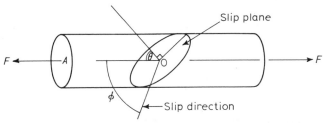

Figure 5.2 Resolved shear stress

For a sample tested in tension, Figure 5.2, the critical resolved shear stress is given by

$$\tau_R = \frac{\text{Load resolved in slip direction}}{\text{Area of slip plane}} = \frac{F\cos\phi}{A/\cos\theta} = \frac{F}{A}\cos\theta\cos\phi$$

(5.4)

where F is the applied force, A the cross-sectional area, θ the angle between the tensile axis and the normal to the slip plane and ϕ is the angle between the tensile axis and the slip direction. The crystallographic data required must be derived from X-ray or other suitable technique. The product ($\cos\theta\cos\phi$) is known as the Schmid factor.

5.4 Tensile deformation of polycrystalline materials

Probably the most useful single test employed by the metallurgist is the tensile test. The test may be conducted over a wide range of strain rates and temperatures. The primary data output are usually in terms of force and extension, but these may be converted to engineering stresses and strains or true stresses and strains if required.

The engineering or nominal stress is defined as

$$S = \frac{F}{A_0} \tag{5.5}$$

where F is the force and A_0 the original cross-sectional area.

The corresponding engineering or conventional strain is defined as

$$e = \frac{L_n - L_0}{L_0} = \frac{\Delta L}{L_0}$$

where L_0 is the original gauge length and L_n an extended length.

Unlike engineering stress and strain values, the true stress and strain are related to the changing cross-sectional area or gauge length respectively.

The true strain may be calculated from summing the increments over small strain intervals

$$\epsilon = \frac{(L_1 - L_0)}{L_0} + \frac{(L_2 - L_1)}{L_1} \ldots + \frac{(L_n - L_{(n-1)})}{L_{(n-1)}} \tag{5.7}$$

or

$$\epsilon = \int_{L_0}^{L_n} \frac{dL}{L} = \ln \frac{L_n}{L_0} \qquad \text{or} \qquad \ln \frac{A_0}{A_n} \tag{5.8}$$

The relationship between engineering strain and true strain is thus

$$e = \frac{(L_n - L_0)}{L_0} = \frac{L_n}{L_0} - 1$$

therefore

$$e + 1 = \frac{L_n}{L_0} = \frac{A_0}{A_n}$$

but

$$\epsilon = \ln \frac{L_n}{L_0} \qquad \text{(Equation (5.8))}$$

therefore

$$\epsilon = \ln (e + 1) \tag{5.9}$$

True stress is related to the changing cross-sectional area, A_n, therefore

$$\sigma = \frac{F}{A_n} = \frac{F A_0}{A_0 A_n} \tag{5.10}$$

It is possible, therefore, to relate the true stress to the engineering stress through the engineering strain

$$\sigma = S (e + 1) \tag{5.11}$$

Many empirical mathematical relationships exist which claim to represent the true stress/true strain curve. The most widely accepted relationship was proposed by Holloman[2] and is applicable from the onset of flow up to the maximum force.

$$\sigma = K\epsilon^n \tag{5.12}$$

where K is the strength coefficient and n is the strain hardening exponent. The fact that many materials are strain rate sensitive may be allowed for

$$\sigma = K'\epsilon^n\dot{\epsilon}^m \tag{5.13}$$

where $\dot{\epsilon}$ is the strain rate and m the strain rate exponent.

It can be argued that other relationships fit the experimental data more completely. One such equation was proposed by Voce[3]

$$\sigma = \sigma_\infty - (\sigma_\infty - \sigma_0) \exp \left(-\frac{\epsilon}{\epsilon_c} \right) \tag{5.14}$$

where σ_∞ is the asymptotic stress, σ_0 the flow stress and ϵ_c the characteristic strain. Voce also argues that Equation (5.14) has more physical significance than Equation (5.12) and certainly it has other benefits such as not predicting an ever increasing stress with strain in contrast with Equation (5.12).

In spite of the better fit to experimental data which Equation (5.14) provides, the Holloman relationship (Equation (5.12)) remains the most popular, probably because it fits data adequately and the constants, especially n, the strain-hardening coefficient, have proved more useful industrially than have the constants in Equation (5.14). From general plastic instability criteria and Considere's[4] construction it can be shown that the true stress at maximum force is numerically equal to n

$$n = \epsilon_{max} \tag{5.15}$$

Derivation of the constants in Equations (5.12) and (5.14) is shown in Figure 5.3 and Considere's construction is shown in Figure 5.4.

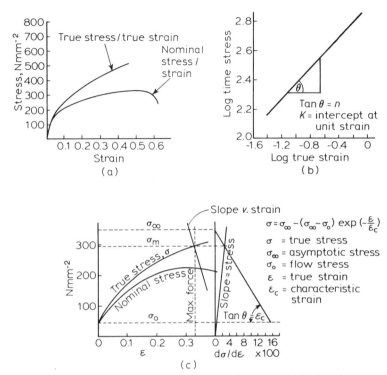

Figure 5.3 Derivation of constants in selected strain hardening functions

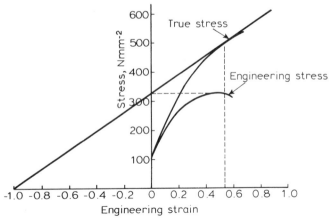

Figure 5.4 Considére's construction

5.4.1 Yield point phenomenon

Most metallic materials when deformed under tensile loading conditions produce an engineering stress–strain curve as shown in Figure 5.3(a). Some, however, show a yield drop effect, Figure 5.5.

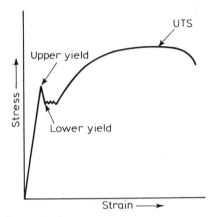

Figure 5.5 Stress–strain plot — yield drop effect

It is possible to derive an expression which relates stress and strain for a small period immediately following yield, much of the original work having been done by Johnston and Gilman[5].

$$\dot{\epsilon}_p = \phi L b v \qquad (5.16)$$

where $\dot{\epsilon}_p$ is the tensile plastic strain rate, ϕ is a factor to convert from shear to tensile, L is the mobile dislocation density, b is the Burgers vector and v the dislocation velocity. The dislocation velocity can be related to the applied stress

$$v = \left(\frac{\sigma}{\sigma_0}\right)^n \qquad (5.17)$$

where v is the dislocation velocity, σ is the applied stress and σ_0 is a constant. Work hardening begins at yield and is allowed for by

$$\frac{d\sigma}{d\epsilon_p} = q \qquad (5.18)$$

where q is the coefficient of work hardening and ϵ_p is the % plastic strain. Equation (5.17) may thus be modified

$$v = \left(\frac{\sigma - q\epsilon_p}{\sigma_0}\right)^n \qquad (5.19)$$

Combining Equations (5.16) and (5.19)

$$\sigma = q\epsilon_p + \sigma_0 \left[\frac{\dot{\epsilon}_p}{\phi L b} \right]^{1/n} \tag{5.20}$$

Dislocation multiplication begins at yield and the total dislocation density ρ is given by

$$\rho = \rho_0 + c\epsilon_p^a \tag{5.21}$$

where ρ_0 is the initial dislocation density and c and a are experimentally derived constants. Therefore

$$L = f\rho \tag{5.22}$$

where f is the constant denoting the fraction of mobile dislocations. From Equations (5.21) and (5.22)

$$L = f(\rho_0 + c\epsilon_p^a) \tag{5.23}$$

hence

$$L = L_0 + fc\epsilon_p^a \tag{5.24}$$

Substituting Equation (5.24) in Equation (5.20) produces the final result

$$\sigma = q\epsilon_p + \sigma_0 \left[\frac{\dot{\epsilon}_p}{\phi b (L_0 + fc\epsilon_p^a)} \right]^{1/n} \tag{5.25}$$

5.5 Three-point bend testing

Tensile testing, although very useful, is not the only means of assessing strength. There are occasions where a bending test leading to the determination of the interlaminar shear stress may be more useful.

Classical continuum theory applied to calculate the interlaminar shear stress (ILSS) gives

$$\tau = \frac{3P}{wt^3}[(t/2)^2 - Y_0^2] \tag{5.26}$$

where P is the applied force, w is the specimen width, t is the specimen thickness and Y_0 is the distance from the neutral plane. The maximum value of the ILSS will be $\frac{3}{4} P/wt$ at the neutral plane and reduce in parabolic manner to zero at the free surfaces.

This theory assumes that a single material is being tested but stress analysis of composite beams can allow for the presence of different materials. For aluminium–steel composite, the thickness,

X, of aluminium with a Young's modulus of E_{al} can be replaced by an equivalent thickness, Y, of steel of Young's modulus E_{st} given by

$$Y = \frac{X E_{al}}{E_{st}} \qquad (5.27)$$

Thus a uniform steel beam of thickness $(Z + Y)$ can represent a composite aluminium–steel beam of thickness $(Z + X)$ where Z is the thickness of the steel in the composite beam. The neutral plane is now at a distance $(Z + Y)/2$ from the loading point and the interface between the steel and aluminium is, therefore, at a distance $(Z - Y)/2$ from the neutral plane. Equation (5.26) may be re-written

$$(\text{ILSS}) \, \tau = \frac{3P}{w(Z + Y)^3} \left[\left(\frac{Z + Y}{2} \right)^2 - \left(\frac{Z - Y}{2} \right)^2 \right] \qquad (5.28)$$

5.6 Hardness

In general terms hardness relates to the resistance to deformation. More specifically with respect to metallic materials, it relates to the resistance to plastic deformation. Hardness is useful for a variety of reasons. The test is quick, simple, requires only a small sample and can, through empirically established relationships, provide a meaningful indication of strength in the absence of tensile data. Its main disadvantage lies in the small sampling area involved which could lead to erroneous conclusions if insufficient tests are conducted.

There are three main types of direct hardness test, namely scratch, rebound or dynamic hardness and indentation hardness. All three types have significant roles to play in materials evaluation but only indentation hardness, the most widely employed in engineering, will be further discussed.

There are several internationally recognized indentation hardness scales, the Brinell and Vickers tests both produce a hardness number by dividing the applied load by the surface area of the impression.

Brinell
(ball indenter) $H_B = \dfrac{P}{(\pi D/2)(D - \sqrt{D^2 - d^2})} = \dfrac{P}{\pi D T} (\text{kg/mm}^2)$

$$(5.29)$$

where P is the applied load (kg), D is the indenter diameter (mm), d is the diameter of impression (mm) and T is the depth of the impression (mm). An alternative expression for Brinell hardness which should be noted with reference to Figure 5.6 is

$$H_B = \frac{P}{(\pi/2) D^2 (1 - \cos \phi)} (\text{kg/mm}^2) \qquad (5.30)$$

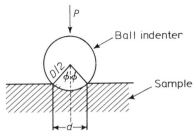

Figure 5.6 Brinell hardness indentation

Vickers hardness is usually determined for a square based diamond indenter, the included angle of 136° being chosen to approximate the most desirable ratio of impression diameter to ball diameter in the Brinell test

$$H_v = \frac{2P\sin(\theta/2)}{L^2} = \frac{1.854\,P}{L^2}\,(\text{kg/mm}^2) \qquad (5.31)$$

where L is the average length of diagonal of impression and θ is the included angle between opposite face of the diamond indenter (136°).

Meyer hardness is similar to Brinell in using a ball indenter but differs from Brinell and Vickers in relating the applied load to the projected area of the impression

$$H_M = \frac{4P}{\pi d^2}(\text{kg/mm}^2) \qquad (5.32)$$

Meyer proposed an empirical relationship between load and impression size

$$P = kd^{n'} \qquad (5.33)$$

where n' is a material constant related to the strain hardening of metal and k is another material constant related to the resistance to penetration. The n' term is of similar nature to n in Equation (5.12), i.e. $n' \simeq n + 2$.

Rockwell hardness, more popular in the United States, is again an indentation system but bases its values on the depth of impression. It has the advantage of high speed and is less operator dependent but requires several scales to cover the full spectrum of engineering materials. The Rockwell hardness numbers are purely arbitrary and do not have units as do the other three scales.

PROGRAMS

Program 5.1: Critical resolved shear stress

The general idea of critical resolved shear stress is outlined in

Section 5.3. This program is written specifically for body-centred-cubic (bcc) metals which may slip on the {110}, {112} or {123} planes with the <111> as the slip direction. From the requested input data on tensile axis and the slip plane to be considered, the program determines the possible slip direction(s) and calculates the Schmid factor(s), i.e. the product ($\cos \theta \cos \phi$) in Equation (5.4).

```
100 INIT
110 PAGE
120 REM 5.1 CRITICAL RESOLVED SHEAR STRESS
140 SET DEGREES
150 G=0
160 DIM U(2),V(2),W(2),S(2)
170 PRINT "ENTER TENSILE AXIS AS H,K,L"
180 INPUT H0,K0,L0
190 PRINT "ENTER SLIP PLANE AS H,K,L"
200 INPUT H,K,L
210 PRINT
220 PRINT "************************************************"
230 PRINT
240 FOR H1=-1 TO 1 STEP 2
250 FOR K1=-1 TO 1 STEP 2
260 FOR L1=-1 TO 1 STEP 2
270 T=(H*H1+K*K1+L*L1)/SQR((H^2+K^2+L^2)*(H1^2+K1^2+L1^2))
280 T=ACS(T)
290 IF T=90 THEN 310
300 GO TO 400
310 IF L1=-1 THEN 400
320 G=G+1
330 U(G)=H1
340 V(G)=K1
350 W(G)=L1
360 IF G>1 THEN 390
370 PRINT "SLIP DIRECTION(S) CONTAINED IN SLIP PLANE"
380 PRINT "-------------------------------------------"
390 PRINT H1,K1,L1
400 NEXT L1
410 NEXT K1
420 NEXT H1
430 IF G=0 THEN 450
440 GO TO 510
450 PRINT
460 PRINT "H,K,L ENTRY IS NOT A SLIP PLANE!-TRY AGAIN!"
470 PRINT
480 PRINT "ENTER R TO RE-RUN FROM START"
490 INPUT R$
500 IF R$="R" THEN 100
510 P=(H*H0+K*K0+L*L0)/SQR((H^2+K^2+L^2)*(H0^2+K0^2+L0^2))
520 PRINT
530 PRINT "ANGLE BETWEEN SLIP PLANE NORMAL AND TENSILE AXIS"
540 PRINT "------------------------------------------------"
550 PRINT ACS(P)
560 PRINT
570 PRINT "ANGLE(S) BETWEEN SLIP DIRN(S) AND TENSILE AXIS"
580 PRINT "----------------------------------------------------"
590 FOR I=1 TO G
600 Q1=H0*U(I)+K0*V(I)+L0*W(I)
610 Q2=SQR((H0^2+K0^2+L0^2)*(U(I)^2+V(I)^2+W(I)^2))
620 Q=Q1/Q2
630 PRINT ACS(ABS(Q))
640 S(I)=ABS(P)*ABS(Q)
650 NEXT I
660 PRINT
670 PRINT "SCHMID FACTOR(S)"
680 PRINT "--------------"
```

```
690 FOR I=1 TO G
700 PRINT S(I)
710 NEXT I
720 PRINT
730 PRINT "**************************************************"
740 PRINT
750 PRINT "IF YOU WISH TO ENTER ANOTHER SLIP PLANE WITH"
760 PRINT "THE SAME TENSILE AXIS,ENTER   S"
770 PRINT "IF YOU WISH TO CHANGE THE TENSILE AXIS,ENTER   R"
780 INPUT A$
790 IF A$="R" THEN 100
800 PAGE
810 G=0
820 GO TO 190
830 END
```

Program notes

(1) The $G=0$ on line 150 is used later to select array storage position(s) for operative slip direction(s) needed in calculation of angle(s) between slip direction(s) and tensile axis, lines 600–630.

(2) Dimensioning of storage arrays in line 160 to 2 is based on the fact that no slip plane can contain more than 2 slip directions in the bcc system. This value may well need to be changed should the program be modified for use with other crystal structures.

(3) Lines 170–200 request and accept necessary data input.

(4) A particular direction can operate only if it is contained within the active slip plane. Lines 240–420 determine and print the appropriate slip directions for the slip plane selected in line 190. The three nested FOR . . . NEXT loops test all possible <111> directions. For a slip direction to be contained in a particular slip plane the angle between the pole of the slip plane and the slip direction must be 90°. The angle is calculated in line 270 and the slip direction subsequently stored if the angle is determined as 90°.

(5) If an invalid plane is entered as a slip plane lines 430–500 detect this and present an option to re-run from the start of the program.

(6) Having determined the operative slip direction(s) the program goes on to calculate and print angles between slip plane normal and tensile axis, angle(s) between slip direction(s) and tensile axis and Schmid factor(s) in lines 510–710.

(7) Lines 750–840 present options for further investigations.

Program 5.2: Tensile analysis

Most tensile tests generate the primary result as a force v. extension curve. From an input of a series of forces at a set extension interval together with the specimen dimensions, the program calculates values of engineering stress, engineering strain, true stress, true strain and log values of the last two parameters. The primary and calculated secondary data are tabulated and a series of graphs plotted to enable comparisons to be made and the values of *n* and *K* in Equation (5.12) to be determined. Equations (5.5–5.12) in Section 5.4 form the basis of the calculation part of the program.

```
100 INIT
110 PAGE
120 REM 5.2 TENSILE ANALYSIS
140 PRINT "CALCULATES FROM FORCE - EXTENSION DATA"
150 PRINT
160 PRINT "ENG.STRESS,ENG.STRAIN,TRUE STRESS,TRUE STRAIN"
170 PRINT "LOG TRUE STRESS,LOG TRUE STRAIN"
180 PRINT
190 PRINT "AND"
200 PRINT
210 PRINT "PLOTS"
220 PRINT
230 PRINT "FORCE/EXTENSION"
240 PRINT "ENG.STRESS/ENG. STRAIN"
250 PRINT "TRUE STRESS/TRUE STRAIN"
260 PRINT "LOG TRUE STRESS/LOG TRUE STRAIN"
270 PRINT "TRUE STRESS and ENG.STRESS/ENG. STRAIN"
280 PRINT "************************************************"
290 PRINT "ENTER NUMBER OF FORCES TO BE PROCESSED"
300 INPUT Z
310 DIM L(Z)
320 PRINT "ENTER FORCES IN NEWTONS"
330 INPUT L
340 PRINT "WIDTH,THICKNESS,LENGTH and INCREMENT in mm's"
350 INPUT H,I,M,P8
360 DIM B(Z),C(Z),D(Z),E(Z),F(Z),X1(Z),Y1(Z),X(Z),Y(Z)
370 REM CALCULATING REQUIRED SECONDARY DATA FROM INPUT DATA
380 J=H*I
390 K=J*M
391 Q=P8
400 G=0
410 N=0
420 G=G+1
430 N=G*P8
440 B(G)=N
450 N=L(G)/J
460 C(G)=N
470 N=Q/M
480 D(G)=N
490 N=L(G)*(M+Q)/K
500 E(G)=N
501 Q=Q+P8
510 N=LOG(D(G)+1)
520 F(G)=N
530 IF G=Z THEN 550
540 GO TO 420
550 FOR R=1 TO Z
560 N=LGT(E(R))
570 X1(R)=N
580 N=LGT(F(R))
590 Y1(R)=N
600 NEXT R
610 REM TABULATING PRIMARY AND CALCULATED DATA
620 PAGE
630 PRINT "MATERIAL         CUSTOMER         DATE
640 PRINT
650 PRINT
660 PRINT USING 670:"FORCE","EXT","E/STS","E/STN","T/STS"
670 IMAGE 5(9A)
680 PRINT USING 690:"KT/STN","L/T/STS","L/T/STN"
690 IMAGE      45X,9A,9A,9A
700 PRINT
```

```
710 FOR R=1 TO Z
720 PRINT USING 730:L(R),B(R),C(R),D(R),E(R),F(R),X1(R),Y1(R)
730 IMAGE(5D,4X,2D.1D,5X,3D,6X,1D.3D,4X,3D,6X,2(1D.3D,4X),-1D.3D)
740 NEXT R
750 COPY
760 REM CHANGE ARRAYS TO PLOT USING SUB 2000 TO X-Y ARRAYS
770 PAGE
780 FOR R=1 TO Z
790 X(R)=B(R)
800 Y(R)=L(R)
810 NEXT R
820 B$="FORCE(Newtons)/EXTENSION(mm's)"
830 CALL "MAX",X,W2,P8
840 CALL "MAX",Y,W4,P8
850 W1=0
860 W3=0
870 GOSUB 2000
880 COPY
890 FOR R=1 TO Z
900 X(R)=D(R)
910 Y(R)=C(R)
920 NEXT R
930 B$="ENG.STRESS(Newton mm -2)/ENG.STRAIN"
940 CALL "MAX",D,W2,P8
950 CALL "MAX",E,W4,P8
960 GOSUB 2000
970 COPY
980 FOR R=1 TO Z
990 X(R)=F(R)
1000 Y(R)=E(R)
1010 NEXT R
1020 B$="TRUE STRESS(Newton mm -2)/TRUE STRAIN"
1030 GOSUB 2000
1040 COPY
1050 FOR R=1 TO Z
1060 X(R)=Y1(R)
1070 Y(R)=X1(R)
1080 NEXT R
1090 B$="LGT TRUE STRESS/LGT TRUE STRAIN"
1100 CALL "MIN",Y1,W1,P8
1110 W3=0
1120 CALL "MAX",X1,W4,P8
1130 W2=0
1140 W4=W4*1.2
1150 GOSUB 2000
1160 COPY
1170 REM SET UP AXES FOR CONSIDERE PLOT -NOT USING SUB 2000
1180 PAGE
1190 WINDOW -1,1,0,E(Z)+40
1200 AXIS 0.2,20
1210 FOR R=1 TO Z
1220 MOVE D(R),E(R)
1230 SCALE 1,1
1240 RMOVE -0.55*1.55,-0.5*1.88
1250 PRINT "*";
1260 RMOVE 0.5*1.55,0.5*1.88
1270 WINDOW -1,1,0,E(Z)+40
1280 NEXT R
1290 MOVE -0.75,E(Z)/2
1300 PRINT "CONSIDERE"
1302 PRINT
1305 PRINT "     TRUE STRESS/ENG.STRAIN";
1310 FOR G=-1 TO 1 STEP 0.2
1320 MOVE G,0
1330 IF ABS(G)<0.1 THEN 1360
1340 PRINT "JJ";G;
1350 GO TO 1370
1360 PRINT "JJ";"0";
```

```
1370 NEXT G
1380 FOR G=20 TO E(Z)+40 STEP 80
1390 MOVE 0,G
1400 PRINT "HHH";G;
1410 NEXT G
1420 FOR R=1 TO Z
1430 MOVE D(R),C(R)
1440 DRAW D(R),C(R)
1450 NEXT R
1460 COPY
1470 PAGE
1480 GO TO 100
2000 REM GENERAL GRAPH PLOTTING ROUTINE
2010 PAGE
2020 N1=10
2030 N2=10
2040 VIEWPORT 10,120,10,90
2050 HOME
2060 PRINT B$
2070 DIM P(8)
2080 P(1)=W1
2090 P(2)=W2
2100 P(3)=N1
2110 P(5)=W3
2120 P(6)=W4
2130 P(7)=N2
2140 REM CALC NEW LIMITS & INTERVALS
2150 P5=3
2160 GOSUB 2380
2170 P5=7
2180 GOSUB 2380
2190 WINDOW P(1),P(2),P(5),P(6)
2200 AXIS P(3),P(7),P(1)+P(3),P(5)+P(7)
2210 FOR G=1 TO Z STEP 1
2220 MOVE X(G),Y(G)
2230 SCALE 1,1
2240 RMOVE -0.5*1.55,-0.5*1.88
2250 PRINT "*";
2260 RMOVE 0.5*1.55,0.5*1.88
2270 WINDOW P(1),P(2),P(5),P(6)
2280 NEXT G
2290 REM LABEL THEM
2300 P5=4
2310 A$="HHH"
2320 GOSUB 2670
2330 P5=8
2340 A$=""
2350 GOSUB 2670
2360 HOME
2370 PRINT
2380 REM P(P5)=MIN NUMBER OF TICS
2390 P1=(P(P5-1)-P(P5-2))/P(P5)
2400 P2=10^INT(LGT(ABS(P1)))
2410 P1=P1/P2
2420 IF P1>2 THEN 2460
2430 IF P1=1 THEN 2500
2440 P2=2*P2
2450 GO TO 2500
2460 IF P1>5 THEN 2490
2470 P2=5*P2
2480 GO TO 2500
2490 P2=10*P2
2500 REM ADJUST DATA MIN
2510 P1=INT(P(P5-2)/P2)
2520 P3=P2*(P1+2)
2530 IF P3<P(P5-2) THEN 2560
2540 P3=P3-P2
2550 GO TO 2530
```

```
2560 P(P5-2)=P3
2570 REM ADJUST DATA MARK
2580 P1=INT(P(P5-1)/P2)
2590 P3=P2*(P1-2)
2600 IF P(P5-1)<P3 THEN 2630
2610 P3=P3+P2
2620 GO TO 2600
2630 P(P5-1)=P3
2640 REM P(P5)=ADJUSTED TIC INTERVAL
2650 P(P5)=P2
2660 RETURN
2670 REM LEBEL AXIS
2680 P4=P(P5-1)
2690 P(4)=P(1)
2700 P(8)=P(5)
2710 P3=ABS(P(P5-3)+P4) MAX ABS(P(P5-2)-P4)
2720 P3=INT(LGT(P3)+1.0E-8)
2730 P2=10^-P3
2740 P1=P(P5-2)-P4/2
2750 P(P5)=P(P5)+P4
2760 IF P(P5)>P1 THEN 2810
2770 MOVE P(4),P(8)
2780 PRINT A$;
2790 PRINT USING "-D.2D,S":P(P5)*P2
2800 GO TO 2750
2810 IF P3=0 THEN 2850
2820 P(P5)=P1
2830 MOVE P(4),P(8)
2840 PRINT USING "2A,+FD,S":" E";P3
2850 RETURN
2860 END
```

Program notes

(1) Lines 120–270 cause a program menu to be printed.

(2) Primary data requests are made, furnished and storage arrays dimensioned in lines 290–360.

(3) Line 370 is one of several REMARK statements used in this program and whilst not commonly employed in other programs are useful in describing the function of a segment of a program.

(4) Cross-sectional area and gauge volume are calculated in lines 380 and 390 respectively. Calculation of other secondary data, with the exception of log values of true stress and true strain, is completed in lines 430–540, where G acts as a counter and N as a temporary variable name for each data calculated prior to placing in a storage array. The log values of true stress and true strain are determined and stored in the FOR . . . NEXT loop, lines 570–620.

(5) The tabulated output is arranged in lines 650–760 using standard PRINT, PRINT USING and IMAGE statements. Line 700 contains a control character K; this is employed to cause printing of the terms in parentheses to be continued on the same line as those in line 680. N.B. This is necessary since there is insufficient space to include all required titles on one program line. (Control characters may vary according to computer used.)

(6) Sub-routine 2000 is a general graph plotting routine which will supply suitable axes with appropriate TIC intervals and labels. A

graph title will also be printed if made available as B$. The minimum and maximum values of X and Y, the plotting variables, must also be available as W1, W2, W3 and W4 respectively.

(7) Lines 780–1180 change the variables to be plotted from their current storage arrays, supply an appropriate title as B$, determine maximum and minimum values as desirable, and instruct a branch to SUB-ROUTINE 2000. On return from the sub-routine a 'hard copy' is made.

(8) In determining the limits for the graphs a CALL statement is used. Should this instruction not be available a short sub-routine to determine maximum and/or minimum values from an array on similar principles to that used in Program 6.1, lines 3230–3340 may be adopted.

(9) In order that direct comparison of engineering stress and strain with true stress and strain may be made, these two graphs are plotted on the same scales by selecting the true stress maximum and the engineering strain maximum, lines 960–970.

(10) The final graph of true engineering stress v. engineering strain, to illustrate the Considere relationship, is set up and processed independently of sub-routine 2000 at lines 1190–1480.

Program 5.3: Yield point phenomena

The program allows investigation of the effects of the stress sensitivity exponent of dislocation velocity, n, and the initial mobile dislocation density, L_0, on the upper/lower yield phenomena. The program is based on the argument put forward in Section 5.4.1 and uses the final Equation (5.25) for calculation of data. The graphics output plots the two functions, making up Equation (5.25), as separate and combined entities. Where an upper and lower yield exist, their values are printed. The data used in the program are typical of that for mild steel. (Units and symbols for data used are listed at the end of the program notes.)

```
100 INIT
110 PAGE
120 REM 5.3 YIELD POINT PHENOMENA
150 DATA 34.4,20,0.02,0.5,2.4E-8,0.1,1.6E+9,0.8
160 READ Q,S0,E2,O,B,F,C,A
170 DIM X(51),Y(51),S(51),E(51)
180 PRINT "WHICH VARIABLE IS TO BE FIXED-n OR L0 ?"
190 INPUT A$
200 IF A$="N" THEN 350
210 PRINT "ENTER FIXED VALUE OF L0 TO BE USED"
220 INPUT L0
230 PRINT "ENTER FIRST VALUE OF n TO BE USED"
240 INPUT N
250 GO TO 480
260 PRINT "ENTER NEXT VALUE OF n TO BE USED"
270 MOVE 10,50
280 PRINT "              OR              "
```

```
290 MOVE 10,30
300 PRINT "ENTER R TO RE-RUN FROM START"
310 MOVE 10,10
320 INPUT B$
330 IF B$="R" THEN 100
340 GO TO 480
350 PRINT "ENTER FIXED VALUE OF n TO BE USED"
360 INPUT N
370 PRINT "ENTER FIRST VALUE OF L0 TO BE USED"
380 INPUT L0
390 GO TO 480
400 PRINT "ENTER NEXT VALUE OF L0 TO BE USED"
410 MOVE 10,50
420 PRINT "                 OR                 "
430 MOVE 10,30
440 PRINT "ENTER R TO RE-RUN FROM START"
450 MOVE 10,10
460 INPUT B$
470 IF B$="R" THEN 100
480 PAGE
490 G=1
500 FOR E1=0 TO 0.5 STEP 0.01
510 I=Q*E1
520 X(G)=I
530 I=S0*(E2/(O*B*(L0+F*C*E1^A)))^(1/N)
540 Y(G)=I
550 S(G)=X(G)+Y(G)
560 E(G)=E1
570 G=G+1
580 NEXT E1
590 WINDOW 0,0.5,0,Y(1)+0.5*Y(1)
600 VIEWPORT 10,50,70,100
610 AXIS
620 MOVE 0,0
630 DRAW E,X
640 WINDOW -0.02,0.5,0,Y(1)+0.5*Y(1)
650 VIEWPORT 70,110,70,100
660 AXIS 0,0,-0.02,0
670 MOVE 0,0
680 DRAW E,Y
690 VIEWPORT 10,50,20,50
700 AXIS 0,0,-0.02,0
710 MOVE 0,0
720 DRAW E,S
730 WINDOW 0,130,0,100
740 VIEWPORT 60,130,0,60
750 MOVE 0,100
760 DIM U(6),V(6)
770 RESTORE 780
780 DATA 0,130,130,0,0,130,0,0,100,100,80,80
790 READ U,V
800 DRAW U,V
810 FOR G=1 TO 4
820 IF S(G+1)<=S(G) THEN 840
830 GO TO 850
840 Y1=S(G+1)
850 NEXT G
860 IF S(2)<=S(1) THEN 880
870 Y1=S(1)
880 IF Y1<S(1) THEN 900
890 GO TO 950
900 MOVE 10,90
910 PRINT "UPPER YIELD =",S(1)
920 MOVE 10,85
930 PRINT "LOWER YIELD =",Y1
940 GO TO 990
950 MOVE 10,90
960 PRINT "NO UPPER/LOWER-YIELD ="
```

```
970 MOVE 20,85
980 PRINT S(1)
990 MOVE 10,70
1000 IF A$="N" THEN 400
1010 GO TO 260
1020 END
```

Program notes

(1) Lines 150–200 input fixed data, dimension storage arrays for plotting variables, and allow selection of variable to be investigated.

(2) Lines 210–470 enable entry of initial control data, and an option to further investigate the same variable or to re-run from start thus enabling the other variable to be investigated. This segment of the program divides equally, lines 210–340 dealing with a fixed value of L_0 and allowing n to be varied whilst lines 350–470 use a fixed value of n and allow L_0 to be changed.

(3) Calculation of the two components making up the stress are calculated for small increments of strain and stored in arrays for subsequent plotting, in lines 490–580.

(4) Plotting of graphs is completed in lines 590–720, redefining window and viewpoint as necessary.

(5) The box format for output of numerical results and instructions for subsequent program use is undertaken by lines 730–800. The RESTORE statement at line 780 is necessary to reset the data pointer.

(6) Upper and lower yield stresses are determined in lines 810–880 and the appropriate titles and values printed within the box format using lines 890–980.

(7) Lines 990–1010 position the cursor and cause an appropriate branch to select continuation instructions.

(8) Units and symbols used in the program – reference Equation (5.25) – are given below

$$q\text{-Q-Kg mm}^{-2},\ \sigma\text{-SO Kg mm}^{-2},\ \epsilon p\text{-E2-mm}^{-1},\ \phi\text{-O},\ b\text{-B-cm}$$

$$f\text{-F},\ c\text{-C-cm}^{-2},\ a\text{-A},\ n\text{-N},\ L_0\text{-L0-cm}^{-2}$$

Program 5.4: Neutral axis and inter-laminar shear stress (ILSS)

For a composite beam, tested in three-point bending, the program calculates the position of the neutral axis together with the ILSS on the neutral plane and materials interface. The output is presented as a combination of numerics and graphics. The program is based on Section 5.5 and principally on Equation (5.28).

```
100 INIT
110 PAGE
120 REM 5.4 NEUTRAL AXIS AND I.L.S.S.
160 E1=6.8*10^4
170 E2=20.6*10^4
```

```
180 PRINT "ENTER THICKNESS STEEL,Al,WIDTH,(mm)and LOAD(N)"
190 INPUT S,A,W,P
200 PRINT "If ALUMINIUM in TENSION enter 2- if STEEL enter 1"
210 INPUT Z
220 PRINT "-------------------------------------------------"
230 PRINT
240 IF Z=1 THEN 370
250 X=A*E1/E2
260 N=(X+S)/2
270 IF N>S THEN 290
280 GO TO 310
290 N1=(N-S)/(E1/E2)+S
300 N=N1
310 T=3*P/(W*(S+X)^3)*(((S+X)/2)^2-((S-X)/2)^2)
320 Q=3*P/(W*(S+X)^3)*((S+X)/2)^2
330 I=N-S
340 GOSUB 2000
350 GOSUB 1000
360 GO TO 180
370 X=S*E2/E1
380 N=(X+A)/2
390 I=N
400 IF N>A THEN 420
410 GO TO 440
420 N1=(N-A)/(E2/E1)+A
430 N=N1
440 T=3*P/(W*(A+X)^3)*(((A+X)/2)^2-((X-A)/2)^2)
450 Q=3*P/(W*(A+X)^3)*((A+X)/2)^2
460 I=N-A
470 GOSUB 2000
480 GOSUB 1000
490 GO TO 180
500 END
1000 VIEWPORT 20,110,20,50
1010 WINDOW 0,90,0,A+S
1020 MOVE 0,0
1030 DRAW 90,0
1040 DRAW 90,A+S
1050 DRAW 0,A+S
1060 DRAW 0,0
1070 MOVE 0,N
1080 DRAW 90,N
1090 MOVE 80,N
1100 PRINT "N/A"
1110 IF Z=2 THEN 1170
1120 MOVE 0,A
1130 PRINT ".............................................    .. "
1140 MOVE 80,A
1150 PRINT "Int"
1160 GO TO 1210
1170 MOVE 0,S
1180 PRINT ".............................................    .. "
1190 MOVE 80,S
1200 PRINT "Int"
1210 IF Z=2 THEN 1270
1220 MOVE 5,A+S/2
1230 PRINT "STEEL"
1240 MOVE 5,A-A/2
1250 PRINT "ALUMINIUM"
1260 GO TO 1310
1270 MOVE 5,S+A/2
1280 PRINT "ALUMINIUM"
1290 MOVE 5,S-S/2
1300 PRINT "STEEL"
1310 MOVE 45,0
1320 PRINT "^"
1330 VIEWPORT 0,130,0,100
1340 WINDOW 0,130,0,100
```

```
1350 MOVE 0,15
1360 PRINT "ENTER C TO CLEAR SCREEN AND RE-RUN"
1370 INPUT C$
1380 IF C$="C" THEN 1400
1390 GO TO 500
1400 PAGE
1410 RETURN
2000 PRINT "Neutral Axis from Load Point=",N,"mm"
2010 PRINT "I.L.S.S. on Neutral Axis =",Q,"Nmm-2"
2020 PRINT "I.L.S.S. on Interface =",T,"Nmm-2"
2030 PRINT "Interface/Neutral distance =",I,"mm"
2040 IF I>0 THEN 2070
2050 PRINT "Interface in TENSION"
2060 GO TO 2080
2070 PRINT "Interface in COMPRESSION"
2080 RETURN
```

Program notes

(1) Since equivalent thicknesses of materials are determined from their moduli these are input at lines 160 and 170.

(2) Data concerning specimen dimensions and configuration are requested and furnished in lines 180–210.

(3) If, for example, the aluminium was chosen as the material in tension, i.e. furthest from the single load point, then lines 250–360 are brought into operation and lines 370–480 would be inoperative. Line 250 expresses aluminium as an equivalent thickness of steel (Equation (5.27)). Since the sample is now 'all steel' the neutral plane will be at the specimen mid-thickness, line 260. If, however, N is greater than S, the thickness of steel, the excess must be converted back into aluminium terms in order to correctly establish the real distance of the neutral plane from the load point, lines 270, 290 and 300. Lines 310–330 calculate the ILSS on the interface, the ILSS on the neutral plane and the distance of interface from the neutral plane respectively.

(4) Had steel been chosen as the material in tension then lines 370–490 would have been operated and lines 250–360 ignored, but the principles in each section are identical.

(5) Sub-routine 2000 is used to print titles and output numerical results whilst sub-routine 1000 presents a graphical representation of the sample with position of the neutral axis.

Program 5.5: Hardness Vickers–ocular to H_v conversion

Having made an impression with either a diamond or ball indenter, the measured size of the indent must be converted to a hardness value in Kg mm^{-2}. This is usually done using a card which relates ocular reading of indent dimension to hardness for the load and microscope objective used. This program does a similar conversion but allows for any ball size or a diamond indenter of standard or non-standard included angle as well as a choice of two objectives.

The program allows for a single, group or range of conversions to be made. The pyramidal diamond indenter conversion is calculated using Equation (5.31) whilst the ball conversions are completed using Equation (5.29), i.e. the Brinell relationship.

```
100 INIT
110 PAGE
120 REM 5.5 HARDNESS VICKERS-OCULAR TO Hv CONVERSION
150 G1=0
160 SET DEGREES
170 PRINT "ENTER LOAD(Kg) AND OBJECTIVE USED(1.5 or 0.666)"
180 INPUT P,O
190 PRINT "BALL or DIAMOND INDENTER USED ?"
200 INPUT A$
210 IF A$="BALL" THEN 260
220 PRINT "ENTER ANGLE OF DIAMOND (STANDARD-136 degrees)"
230 INPUT D
240 C$="degree "
250 GO TO 290
260 PRINT "ENTER DIAMETER OF BALL(mm)"
270 INPUT D
280 C$="mm"
290 PRINT "SINGLE(I),GROUP(G)orRANGE(R) TO BE CONVERTED ?"
300 INPUT B$
310 PAGE
320 IF B$="I" THEN 580
330 IF B$="G" THEN 450
340 PRINT "ENTER OCULAR RANGE TO BE CONVERTED ";
345 PRINT "eg 200,230(max range 40)"
350 INPUT R1,R2
360 DIM H1(R2-R1+1),L1(R2-R1+1)
370 Y=R2-R1+1
380 FOR L=R1 TO R2
390 G1=G1+1
400 L1(G1)=L
410 GOSUB 1000
420 H1(G1)=H
430 NEXT L
440 GO TO 640
450 PRINT "ENTER No OF OCULARS TO BE CONVERTED (40 max)"
460 INPUT Z
470 Y=Z
480 DIM H1(Z),L1(Z),L2(Z)
490 PRINT "ENTERS OCULARS TO BE CONVERTED"
500 INPUT L2
510 FOR X=1 TO Z
520 L=L2(X)
530 GOSUB 1000
540 H1(X)=H
550 L1(X)=L
560 NEXT X
570 GO TO 640
580 PRINT "ENTER OCULAR TO BE CONVERTED"
590 INPUT L
600 Y=1
610 GOSUB 1000
620 H1=H
630 L1=L
640 PAGE
650 PRINT "LOAD ";P;" Kg",D;C$;A$
660 PRINT
670 PRINT "OCULAR","HARDNESS","OCULAR","HARDNESS"
680 IF Y=1 THEN 800
690 Y1=Y
700 IF INT(Y/2)<>Y/2 THEN 720
710 GO TO 730
720 Y=Y-1
```

```
730 FOR X=1 TO Y STEP 2
740 PRINT L1(X),INT(H1(X)),L1(X+1),INT(H1(X+1))
750 NEXT X
760 IF Y1=Y THEN 810
770 Y=Y+1
780 PRINT L1(Y),INT(H1(Y))
790 GO TO 810
800 PRINT L1,INT(H1)
810 MOVE 0,20
820 PRINT "ENTER R FOR REPEAT RUN or S TO RUN FROM START"
830 INPUT D$
840 G1=0
850 IF D$="S" THEN 100
860 IF D$="R" AND B$="R" THEN 340
870 IF D$="R" AND B$="I" THEN 580
880 IF D$="R" AND B$="G" THEN 450
890 END
1000 IF O=0.666 THEN 1020
1010 GO TO 1040
1020 L3=L*1.0E-3
1030 GO TO 1050
1040 L3=L*0.0025
1050 IF A$="BALL" THEN 1080
1060 H=2*P*SIN(D/2)/L3^2
1070 GO TO 1090
1080 H=P/(PI*(D/2)*(D-SQR(D^2-L3^2)))
1090 RETURN
```

Program notes

(1) G1 set to zero in line 150 is to be used as a counter if a range of conversions is selected, see line 390. It is reset to zero after use at line 840.

(2) Lines 170–330 present a series of requests for data the answers to which determine which routing should be followed.

(3) A range of conversions is dealt with in lines 340–440, a group in lines 450–570 and an individual conversion in lines 580–630. In each case sub-routine 1000 is used to make the hardness calculation from the ocular input(s) for the selected objective and type of indenter.

(4) Lines 640–890 are concerned with output for all three options, i.e. range, group or single conversion. This segment ends, lines 810–880 by presenting re-run options.

PROBLEMS

(5.1) Use Program 5.1 to answer the following questions

(a) Which <111> direction(s) are contained in the following slip planes (123), (121), (101), ($\bar{1}$01)

(b) Which of the following combinations gives the lowest Schmid factor?

 (i) [100] tensile axis (123) slip plane

 (ii) [113] tensile axis ($\bar{1}$12) slip plane

 (iii) [111] tensile axis ($1\bar{1}0$) slip plane

 (iv) [110] tensile axis ($3\bar{2}1$) slip plane

(5.2) Extend program 5.1 so that it is possible to explore a face-centred-cubic (fcc) material in addition to the present body-centred-cubic-ones. In fcc metals slip takes place on the {111} planes in the <110> directions.

(5.3) At present the tensile axis is entered as a direction, e.g. [110]. Modify Program 5.1 to determine the Schmid factors for a range of angles either side of a specified direction.

(5.4) Data are given below for tensile tests conducted on copper, 90/10 gilding metal and 70/30 brass up to the maximum load. Add to the end of the existing Program 5.2 the linear regression sub-routine 1000–1880 of Program 3.1 using an APPEND (MERGE) statement or type in as necessary. Utilize the sub-routine to evaluate n and K in Equation (5.12) and add the necessary output statements. Note how n varies with zinc addition to copper. Knowing that $\epsilon_{max} = n$, Equation (5.15), arrange the modified program to print the % elongation to plastic instability for an ideal test piece.

Data for tensile tests (50 mm gauge lengths)

Specimen dimensions: Brass — width 10.55 mm thickness 1.82 mm
Gilding metal — width 9.40 mm thickness 1.84 mm
Copper — width 9.75 mm thickness 1.61 mm

| | Force Nmm^{-2} | | |
Extension (mm)	Copper	Gilding metal	70/30 brass
2	1800	2275	2950
4	2400	3100	3700
6	2725	3600	4200
8	2950	4050	4700
10	3100	4300	5050
12	3175	4450	5400
14	3250	4575	5675
16	3260	4650	5875
18	3275	4700	6050
20			6100
22			6200
24			6250
26			6300

(5.5) It can be argued that Equation (5.14) fits tensile test data better than does Equation (5.12). Write a program to analyse tensile data on the basis of Equation (5.14).

(5.6) Some materials are strain rate sensitive, Equation (5.13). Write a program which allows the effects of changing K, $\dot{\epsilon}$, n and m to be investigated. The tabulated output format of Program 5.2 could be utilized with little modification.

(5.8) Use Program 5.3 to examine the effects of n and L_0, Equation

(5.25). Suggested ranges for n and L_0 are 10–300 and $10^2 - 10^7$ cm^{-2} respectively.

(5.9)

(a) After becoming familiar with Program 5.4, change the appropriate data and print statements to investigate a different couple.

(b) Modify the program to enable materials names and moduli to be entered during program running, i.e. make it general rather than specific.

(5.10) Modify Program 5.5 so that, when a range of conversions is selected, the output format is as for a standard Vickers card. This will allow a larger range to be dealt with and give experience in the use of formatting statements.

(5.11) Write a program which compares Brinell and Meyer hardnesses, Equations (5.29) and (5.32), for the same diameter of impression.

References

(1) Schmid, E., *Z. Electrochem.*, **37**, 447, (1931).

(2) Holloman, J. H., *Trans., AIME*, **162**, p. 268, (1945).

(3) Voce, E., 'A practical strain hardening function', *Metallurgia*, (May 1955).

(4) Considere, A., *Ann. ponts et Chaussees*, **9**, Ser. 6, pp. 574–775, (1885).

(5) Johnston and Gilman, *J. App. Phys.*, **30**, 129, (1959).

Bibliography

Dieter, G. E., *Mechanical Metallurgy*, McGraw-Hill Kogakusha Ltd, (1976).

Van Vlack, L. H., *Materials Science for Engineers*, Addison-Wesley Pub. Co., (1982).

Chapter 6

Materials properties comparisons

ESSENTIAL THEORY

6.1 Introduction

There are a number of reasons why it is convenient to be able to compare the characteristics of materials over quite a range of properties. The designer wishes to select the best material for a given application. Value analysis may require a reduction in costs for an established product which would involve a comparison of competitive materials. Failure of a material in a particular application may require an alternative to be sought. There may be a problem over the availability of particular materials and alternatives will need to be found to fill a shortage in supply. In addition to this the comparison of the properties of materials has educational benefits and a convenient and interactive way of comparing the properties of materials enables a student to gain considerable insight into the characteristics of common materials. A number of approaches have been made to the systematic comparison and selection of alloys to fit particular applications. Some use a book or series of books, while others use a computer.

The present chapter allows the analysis of a collection of data to be made chiefly as a teaching aid to illustrate to students the materials available, the variety of their properties and the combinations of characteristics that are available or impossible to achieve with real materials. The advent of the small desktop computer with magnetic tape cartridge enables this to be done in a very compact and portable way and yet with enough detail for it to be of some value and interest.

The present program enables twelve representative properties of a number of common materials to be compared in a variety of ways. As written, it contains information on 75 materials, but that number could be extended considerably without using an excessive amount of memory. Data on about 100 materials could be stored and manipulated by a popular 32K 'hobby' computer. The program covers a wide range of materials but specialized forms could easily be written based on the present model to cover heat-treatable steels or high-temperature materials or electrical alloys or casting alloys. In this case different data would be stored for a more limited range of materials and would be analysed under more specialist headings.

Materials can be compared in a number of ways; one can for instance use density, strength and hardness all of which are direct properties of the material, or one can use derived properties such as specific modulus (modulus/density) or specific strength (strength/density), where two direct properties of the material are associated in some mathematical formula to achieve the derived property. Having chosen the property, sometimes one is interested in the material which has the maximum value of that property, sometimes the material with the minimum value of that property and occasionally with all the materials whose property value falls within a certain range. Another way of comparing materials is to rank them into a sequence or order of merit based on a number of characteristics. The user specifies which property is of most importance, which is second and which is third and so on, and then an order of merit is produced for the range of materials under consideration. Both of these methods of selection are addressed in this chapter and a straightforward program section is given to cover each particular type.

The list of direct properties chosen to characterize the metals and alloys is as follows:

1. Young's modulus GN/m^2 (GPa)
2. Density tonne/m^3 (Mg/m^3)
3. Cost £/tonne
4. Hardness Vickers
5. Proof stress MN/m^2 (MPa)
6. UTS MN/m^2 (MPa)
7. Tensile elongation (%)
8. Plane strain fracture toughness $MN/m^{\frac{3}{2}}$ (MPa $\sqrt{m}$)
9. Fatigue stress 10^7 cycles MN/m^2 (MPa)
10. Resistivity n ohm m
11. Room temperature Charpy energy J
12. Solidus temperature (°C)

This list is by no means exhaustive but it gives a good cross-section of the overall characteristics of a given alloy. One could also include creep, service temperature, hardenability for steels and other properties relating to specific areas of application.

These twelve properties can be combined to produce a number of derived properties, the five selected here being:

Specific strength, MNm/tonne
Specific elastic modulus, GNm/tonne
Cost per unit of strength, £/MNm
Critical crack size, mm
Weight per unit of electrical conductivity, kg

The specific strength of a material can be defined as the tensile load that can be sustained by a bar of unit length and mass. For a bar of unit length, cross sectional area A, strength σ and density ρ we have

Tensile force $= A \times \sigma$
Mass $= A \times \rho$
Force/unit mass $= \sigma/\rho =$ specific strength

Similar reasoning leads to a definition of specific modulus as Y/ρ where Y is the Young's modulus of the material.

The cost per unit of strength is (following Alexander[1]) a measure of the cost of a bar 1 m long that will support unit force without deformation of fracture.

Tensile force $= A \times \sigma$
Mass $= A \times \rho$ cost $= A \times \rho \times C$

where $C =$ cost/unit mass

$$\text{Cost/unit force} = \frac{C \times \rho}{\sigma}$$

In linear elastic fracture mechanics the critical crack size can be calculated for an infinite plate with a centre crack of length $2\,c$, as

$$2\,c = \frac{8}{\pi}\left(\frac{K_{1c}^{2}}{\sigma_y}\right)$$

where $\sigma_y =$ yield stress and $K_{1c} =$ plane strain fracture toughness. This represents the maximum length of crack that is stable in such a plate at half the yield stress of the material. Larger cracks will be stable at lower values of applied stress while smaller cracks will be tolerable at higher values of applied stress. Half the yield stress is chosen as a reasonable value for the application of linear elastic fracture mechanics as plastic zone corrections for ratios of applied stress to yield stress greater than 0.5 begin to get significant. Calculation of the critical crack size for a standard geometry gives a clear indication of the tolerance of a material to flaws.

Other characteristics concern electrical conductivity. The mass per unit conductivity refers to a bar of length 1 m with conductivity of 10^{-6} ohm^{-1}. The value is calculated by multiplying the electrical resistivity by the density and is an important property for instance in the choice of suspended overhead electrical conductors. For a bar of unit length

Conductivity of bar $= A/S$
Mass of bar $= A \times \rho$
Mass/unit conductivity $= S \times \rho$

6.2 Order of merit classification

Materials often have to be chosen to meet a situation where more than one property is important. Usually one property is of primary importance but there may be two others which, although they are of less importance, still contribute to the choice between the materials. In this case there is a need to include some assessment based on all three of the properties in selecting between materials. In order to do this a figure of merit can be calculated for each material. The maximum value of this figure is set at 100 and up to 50 is contributed by the first property chosen, up to 33.3 by the second property chosen and up to 16.7 by the third. Thus, the properties are ranked in importance in the ratios 3 to 2 to 1. If a material had the highest value of all three properties among the materials considered it would score 100 points. The formula used is as follows

$$Q_A = 3 \times \frac{100}{6} \times \frac{K_A}{K_{max}} + 2 \times \frac{100}{6} \times \frac{L_A}{L_{max}} + \frac{100}{6} \times \frac{M_A}{M_{max}}$$

where Q_A is the merit number, K, L and M are three properties, the subscript A refers to material A and the subscript 'max' refers to the maximum value of that property among all the materials considered. It is important to recognize that the merit number calculated is valid only for the particular sequence of properties specified and the group of materials considered. If a larger number of materials were scanned and the maximum values of K, L or M were different, then the scores obtained by the given material would also be different. However, the order of merit classification does offer a method of specifying in a collection of properties and assessing materials on the basis of these properties rather than one individual property.

An advantage of using a computer in an analysis of this sort is that one can specify how many properties are important in any given case and then rank them in order if the program is of a sufficiently general kind. The example given above of three properties is a simple illustration, but the program described here enables any number of properties up to 10 to be chosen with any order of preference yet the program is only slightly longer than a program that only allows three properties to be selected.

In the general case, if N properties are selected, the formula becomes

$$Q_A = 100 \times \frac{2}{N(N+1)} \times \left(N \times \frac{K_A}{K_{max}} + (N-1) \times \frac{L_A}{L_{max}} + (N-2)\frac{M_A}{M_{max}} \ldots\right)$$

The weighting factors for, say, six properties are 6,5,4,3,2 and 1 and the sum of the individual terms is divided by $\frac{1}{2}N(N+1)$ which is the sum of all the numbers $1 + 2 + 3 \ldots N$.

The assessment of materials by order of merit is of course critically dependent on the weighting factors used. It is convenient to use the weighting system proposed here for simplicity of computation but for three properties weighting factors of 0.5, 0.333 and 0.167 may not be the most suitable. If this is so the program enables other weighting factors for three properties to be tested by nominating four properties and using the same one twice. The weighting factors for four properties are 0.4, 0.3, 0.2 and 0.1. By combining these in various ways the weighting factors given in Table 6.1 may be achieved. Nominating five properties and using two of them twice or one three times gives a still wider range of weighting factors.

Table 6.1

Order of precedence	Weighting factors		
	A	B	C
Three properties			
A B C	0.5	0.333	0.167
Four properties			
A A B C	0.7	0.2	0.1
A B A C	0.6	0.3	0.1
A B C A	0.5	0.3	0.2
B A A C	0.5	0.4	0.1
A B C B	0.4	0.4	0.2
A B C C	0.4	0.3	0.3

6.3 The data

At first sight it would seem to be a simple problem to obtain property data on a series of well known alloys. There are lists of properties of such alloys in various reference volumes and apparently all one needs to do is to collect the data together. However, there are some problems in doing this. The first problem is that although data may be available from many sources for a given material, the data are often not strictly comparable in that the alloy may be in a different metallurgical condition for, say, the toughness data from its condition for the tensile data. This means that the sets of properties that are dependent on micro-structure are not inter-changeable and do not all refer to the same materials under the same conditions. Physical properties such as density, Young's modulus and solidus temperature are fairly straightforward and are not subject to this difficulty. It is necessary to have values of hard-ness, proof stress, ultimate tensile strength, tensile elongation, fracture toughness, fatigue strength and room temperature Charpy impact energy, all of which relate to the same batch of material in identical metallurgical condition, and such data are difficult to obtain. Another problem is that specifications sometimes call for minimum properties of a certain type whereas the designer may require typical properties or vice versa. Certainly typical properties are of more interest to the student as they illustrate much better the influence of strengthening mechanisms in the various alloy systems. In order to try to cover some of these points in specific cases a range of metallurgical conditions could be given for one material. For instance 70/30 brass could be quoted cast, worked and annealed with three different grain sizes. A particular steel could be quoted in four heat treated conditions and so on. This enables comparative information to be obtained about the way in which various proper-ties of a given material are related to each other. The range of properties available from a given material can also be found.

The most difficult property to find values for is fracture tough-ness. This is partly because it is a new property, partly because it is quite expensive to measure, partly because standards usually do not call for particular values of fracture toughness and partly because many ductile materials such as pure copper or mild steel do not fail under fast fracture conditions and so will not have a determinable value for K_{IC}. The advanced high-strength alloys may be specified on the basis of fracture toughness but it is quite unusual for the common popular materials to be specified in this way. Some time has been spent in collecting fracture toughness data for aluminium alloys, titanium alloys and steels but the majority of heat treatable steels do not have values readily available.

Because of these problems it is not possible to find data for every one of the twelve properties for each of the materials of interest. There will therefore be some gaps in the table of data. The method adopted to cope with these gaps is to enter a zero for any property whose value is not obtainable. The computer is then instructed to treat a zero as 'no information' rather than as a property value. Hence comparisons of properties are only possible for those materials for which a non-zero value of property has been entered. For this reason a request for a range of critical crack sizes only pro-duces a few results because data are not available for both fracture toughness and yield stress for all the materials.

In comparing properties of polymers and ceramics with those of metals, certain problems arise. The yield stress is much less easily defined for polymers than for metals and the solidus temperature has no exact parallel. Ball indentation hardness values have been used for polymers and the upper temperature limit for continuous use is quoted in place of the solidus temperature ASTM standard D 638 is used for the tensile data and D 256 for the impact data which have been converted to equivalent Charpy values. The values of the mechanical properties quoted are average values but considerable variation exists due to formulation, molecular weight, processing and thermal history. The values should therefore only be used as a guide. The rubbers quoted contain 50 phr carbon black. The carbon fibre expoxide contains 60 volume percent carbon fibres and the properties are measured in the fibre direction. Ceramics exhibit very little ductility so the yield and ultimate stresses are quoted as equal. Strength is measured in bending and the bend strength is roughly twice the tensile strength which is extremely difficult to measure directly. For this reason for ceramics the tensile strengths quoted are half the bend strengths. Costs at the end of 1983 have been quoted in every case as a guide to the comparison between materials.

PROGRAM

Rather than use a series of short programs it was felt preferable to write one long program which covers all the aspects described in the earlier part of the chapter and which allows comparisons to be made between a number of common materials. Although the total program length is some 300 lines, the program has been written in sections and will be described in those sections, each section being some 60 lines long. The sections cover the reading of the property data, the selection of the particular direct or indirect property required, the determination of the material which has the maximum of given property or minimum of that property or those materials falling within a given range of the property and the order of merit rating based on a selection of a number of properties. Two subroutines are used to produce suitable output from various parts of the main program and they will be described finally.

```
100 REM 6.1 MATERIAL PROPERTY COMPARISONS
110 PRINT @32,18:3
120 DELETE A,F,X,B,C
130 F=75
140 REM*****************************************READ DATA FILE
145 DATA "AL 1100    ANN","AL 1100 H14"
150 DATA "AL MG 5083 ANN","AL MG 5083 H34","AL MN 3003 ANN"
155 DATA "AL CU 2014 T6","AL MG SI 6061 T6","AL ZN MG 7039"
160 DATA "AL ZN MG CU 7075 T6","AL 12SI 413"
```

```
165 DATA "MG AZ91B AS CAST","MG AZ31B ANN"
170 DATA "COPPER OFHC ANNEALED","COPPER OFHC WORKED"
175 DATA "BRASS ANNEALED","BRASS WORKED 50%"
180 DATA "60/40 BRASS EXTD","CU 1%CR ST CW AGED"
185 DATA "CU 2%BE ST AGED","GUN METAL 5SN 5ZN 5PB","CU 30%NI"
190 DATA "AL BRONZE 9AL 2FE","PHOSPHOR BRONZE"
195 DATA "LEAD 99.9","PB 6SB EXTD","TIN PURE ALPHA"
200 DATA "TI CP GRADE 2","TI-6-4 ANN","ZINC CP ROLLED"
205 DATA "NI 200 ANN","NI 33CU","NI 16CR 6FE INCONEL 600"
210 DATA "NIMONIC 105","GREY CAST IRON","SPHEROIDAL CAST IRON"
215 DATA "MALL. CAST IRON","MILD STEEL","150M19 STEEL NORMSD"
220 DATA "150M19 STEEL Q&T","823M30 STEEL NORMALISED"
225 DATA "823M30 STEEL Q&T","H C SPRING STEEL Q&T"
230 DATA "H S L A STEEL","BS 1 TOOL STEEL"
235 DATA "18/8 STAINLESS"
240 DATA "HY80 STEEL Q&T"
245 DATA "MARAGING STEEL 1400"
250 DATA "L D POLYETHYLENE","H D POLYETHYLENE","POLYPROPYLENE"
255 DATA "POLYOXYMETHYLENE","NYLON 6-6","POLYVINYLCHLORIDE"
260 DATA "POLYSTYRENE","A B S (HIGH IMPACT)","POLYCARBONATE"
265 DATA "EPOXIDE","P M M A","PHENOL FORMALDEHIDE"
270 DATA "NATURAL RUBBER","S B R","POLYCHLOROPRENE"
275 DATA "POLYESTER S M C","CARBON FIBRE EPOXIDE"
280 DATA "ELECTRICAL PORCELAIN","GLASS","GLASS-CERAMIC"
285 DATA "ALUMINA","SILICA","TITANIA"
290 DATA "ZIRCONIA","BORON CARBIDE","SILICON CARBIDE"
295 DATA "TUNGSTEN CARBIDE","SILICON NITRIDE HOT PRESSED"
300 DATA 69,2.71,24,34,90,0,34,29.2,0,643,45,1550
305 DATA 69,2.71,34,117,124,0,48,29.7,0,643,20,1550
310 DATA 70.3,2.66,68,145,290,0,0,59.5,0,574,22,1585
315 DATA 70.3,2.66,105,285,345,0,160,59.5,0,574,9,1585
320 DATA 70,2.73,30,42,110,0,48,34,0,643,35,1550
325 DATA 72.4,2.8,140,414,483,31,125,43,0,507,13,2050
330 DATA 68.3,2.7,100,276,310,0,97,40,0,582,17,1750
335 DATA 70,2.78,113,310,370,0,0,46,20,0,15,2680
340 DATA 71,2.8,157,503,572,28,159,52.2,0,532,11,2740
345 DATA 71,2.66,68,145,295,0,130,55.6,0,575,2.5,1130
350 DATA 45,1.81,66,150,230,0,97,170,2.7,470,3,2260
355 DATA 45,1.77,59,150,255,0,0,92,4,532,21,31500
360 DATA 118,8.94,45,62,216,0,0,17,48,1083,60,1300
365 DATA 118,8.94,115,324,386,0,62,18,0,1083,4,1300
370 DATA 105,8.52,65,78,325,0,114,62,58,930,65,1340
375 DATA 105,8.52,200,386,575,0,150,62,0,930,2,1340
380 DATA 105,8.39,150,385,540,0,0,62,0,0,10,1520
385 DATA 130,8.89,160,433,510,0,193,22,20,1070,20,3200
390 DATA 130,8.25,390,930,1320,0,310,68,0,886,3,10600
395 DATA 83,8.83,65,93,250,0,76,0,0,855,20,1170
400 DATA 150,8.94,175,595,636,0,220,360,0,1170,5,2600
405 DATA 115,7.65,205,390,640,0,200,144,0,1040,24,0
410 DATA 105,8.77,0,772,926,0,0,0,0,832,4,2830
415 DATA 14,11.34,5,7,17.5,0,0,206,15,326,50,530
420 DATA 16,10.88,11,0,23,0,8.3,253,0,252,65,730
425 DATA 44,7.3,4,12,0,0,2.9,110,44,232,70,12700
430 DATA 103,4.5,210,360,430,0,0,500,150,1665,20,14500
435 DATA 110,4.43,370,825,895,75,500,1710,27,1604,10,29000
440 DATA 97,7.18,45,0,150,0,17,61,0,419,65,1200
445 DATA 204,8.89,114,148,462,0,228,95,163,1435,47,9210
450 DATA 179,8.83,137,230,540,0,231,510,160,1299,44,6520
455 DATA 207,8.42,150,300,650,0,270,1030,160,1355,40,7110
460 DATA 189,8.01,390,815,1140,0,350,1310,16,1290,12,21500
465 DATA 145,7.3,280,260,400,0,0,640,0,0,1,1250
470 DATA 169,7.1,156,289,420,0,0,500,18,0,12,1900
475 DATA 169,7.35,132,181,290,0,0,300,16,0,6,2500
480 DATA 210,7.85,127,280,430,133,220,140,100,1493,40,250
485 DATA 210,7.85,180,290,550,0,260,220,80,1490,18,350
490 DATA 210,7.85,216,570,700,186,530,220,100,1490,27,380
495 DATA 208,7.85,300,500,900,0,300,260,40,0,10,640
500 DATA 208,7.83,340,850,1100,0,0,260,50,0,12,670
```

```
505 DATA 212,7.83,292,680,945,0,460,200,3,1380,4,390
510 DATA 210,7.85,202,600,700,0,0,0,130,0,16,575
515 DATA 0,7.87,625,1240,1625,0,0,340,15,1500,8,1960
520 DATA 208,7.94,150,230,550,0,0,740,90,1520,45,1150
525 DATA 207,7.84,230,550,620,0,0,300,100,0,25,720
530 DATA 180,8.37,450,1400,1460,145,450,950,27,1430,14,9500
535 DATA 0.2,0.92,1.38,8,15,0,0,0,0,0.5,85,800,550
540 DATA 1,0.95,5.46,30,30,0,0,0,0,0.1,120,600,650
545 DATA 1.4,0.9,7.4,32,33,0,0,0,0,0.05,150,600,550
550 DATA 3,1.43,14.3,0,69,0,0,0,0,0.1,175,40,1000
555 DATA 2,1.24,7.4,57,80,0,0,0,0,0.1,200,200,1500
560 DATA 2.6,1.4,11.2,48,50,0,0,0,0,0.025,80,20,500
565 DATA 3.4,1.05,11.7,0,50,1.05,0,0,0,0.01,100,2.5,650
570 DATA 2,1.01,0,0,34,2.7,0,0,0,0.3,85,30,2000
575 DATA 2.4,1.2,9.96,0,60,0,0,0,0,0.5,165,125,900
580 DATA 2.4,1.2,0,0,60,0,0,0,0,0.01,0,5,1000
585 DATA 3.2,1.19,17.6,0,65,0,0,0,0,0.02,90,5,900
590 DATA 6,1.3,19.4,0,55,0,0,0,0,0.01,0,1,500
595 DATA 0.0175,1.12,0,0,30,0,0,0,0,0,600,790
600 DATA 0.0135,1.02,0,0,20,0,0,0,0,0,500,835
605 DATA 0.006,1.42,0,0,27,0,0,0,0,0,800,1000
610 DATA 17,2,0,0,150,0,0,0,0.5,0,1,800
615 DATA 220,1.55,0,0,1400,0,0,0,0,0,0.8,20000
620 DATA 70,0,700,40,0,0,0,1.0E+19,0,1180,0,50
625 DATA 70,2.5,400,50,0,0,0,1.0E+22,0,450,0,0
630 DATA 100,2.4,0,100,0,0,0,0,0,0,0,0
635 DATA 380,3.9,2000,150,0,0,0,1.0E+22,0,1950,0,250
640 DATA 70,2.6,800,18,0,0,0,1.0E+18,0,1200,0,10
645 DATA 100,0,580,50,0,0,0,1.0E+19,0,0,0,1000
650 DATA 160,5.6,1250,70,0,8,0,1.0E+13,0,1870,0,3000
655 DATA 460,2.5,2800,180,0,0,0,4000000,0,1200,0,0
660 DATA 350,3.2,2700,250,0,4,0,500000,0,1600,0,0
665 DATA 700,0,2800,180,0,0,0,100,0,0,0,0
670 DATA 160,3.1,2000,400,0,5,0,1.0E+20,0,1650,0,10000
800 P=0
810 DIM A(F,12),B(F)
820 FOR I=1 TO F
830 READ A$
840 NEXT I
850 FOR I=1 TO F
860 FOR J=1 TO 12
870 READ A(I,J)
880 NEXT J
890 NEXT I
900 GO TO 1000
910 GOSUB 4000
1000 PAGE
1010 PRINT "0 LIST MATERIALS"
1020 PRINT "1 YOUNGS MODULUS GN/m^2"
1030 PRINT "2 DENSITY tonne/m^3"
1040 PRINT "3 HARDNESS VICKERS"
1050 PRINT "4 PROOF STRESS MN/m^2"
1060 PRINT "5 U T S MN/m^2"
1070 PRINT "6 FRACTURE TOUGHNESS MN/m^3/2"
1080 PRINT "7 FATIGUE STRESS MN/m^2"
1090 PRINT "8 RESISTIVITY n ohm.m"
1100 PRINT "9 IMPACT RT J"
1110 PRINT "10 SOLIDUS TEMP C"
1120 PRINT "11 SPECIFIC MODULUS GNm/tonne"
1130 PRINT "12 COST/UNIT STRENGTH £/MNm"
1140 PRINT "13 SPECIFIC STRENGTH MNm/tonne"
1150 PRINT "14 CRITICAL CRACK SIZE mm"
1160 PRINT "15 WEIGHT PER UNIT CONDUCTIVITY kg"
1170 PRINT "16 PROPERTIES OF ONE MATERIAL"
1180 PRINT "17 ORDER OF MERIT"
1190 PRINT "18 STOP"
1200 PRINT
1210 PRINT "ENTER REQUIRED PROPERTY  GGGGGG";
```

```
1220 INPUT P
1230 IF P=0 OR P=16 THEN 910
1240 IF P=18 THEN 3560
1250 IF P=17 THEN 2000
1260 IF P=15 THEN 1700
1270 IF P=14 THEN 1620
1280 IF P=13 THEN 1540
1290 IF P=12 THEN 1380
1300 IF P=11 THEN 1460
1310 IF P>18 THEN 1000
1320 REM**********************ROUTINE FOR DIRECT PROPERTIES
1330 FOR I=1 TO F
1340 B(I)=A(I,P)
1350 NEXT I
1360 GO TO 3010
1370 REM**********************COST/UNIT STRENGTH
1380 FOR I=1 TO F
1390 IF A(I,5)<>0 THEN 1420
1400 B(I)=0
1410 GO TO 1430
1420 B(I)=A(I,12)*A(I,2)/A(I,5)
1430 NEXT I
1440 GO TO 3010
1450 REM**********************SPECIFIC MODULUS
1460 FOR I=1 TO F
1470 IF A(I,2)<>0 THEN 1500
1480 B(I)=0
1490 GO TO 1510
1500 B(I)=A(I,1)/A(I,2)
1510 NEXT I
1520 GO TO 3010
1530 REM**********************SPECIFIC STRENGTH
1540 FOR I=1 TO F
1550 IF A(I,2)<>0 THEN 1580
1560 B(I)=0
1570 GO TO 1590
1580 B(I)=A(I,5)/A(I,2)
1590 NEXT I
1600 GO TO 3010
1610 REM**********************CRITICAL CRACK SIZE
1620 FOR I=1 TO F
1630 IF A(I,4)<>0 THEN 1660
1640 B(I)=0
1650 GO TO 1670
1660 B(I)=2000/PI*(A(I,6)/A(I,4))^2
1670 NEXT I
1680 GO TO 3010
1690 REM**********************WEIGHT/UNIT CONDUCTIVITY
1700 FOR I=1 TO F
1710 B(I)=A(I,8)*A(I,2)
1720 NEXT I
1730 GO TO 3010
2000 REM*************************THREE PROPERTY COMPARISON
2010 FOR I=1 TO F
2020 IF A(I,2)=0 THEN 2040
2030 A(I,2)=1/A(I,2)
2040 IF A(I,12)=0 THEN 2060
2050 A(I,12)=1/A(I,12)
2060 IF A(I,8)=0 THEN 2080
2070 A(I,8)=1/A(I,8)
2080 NEXT I
2090 PAGE
2100 DELETE C,V
2110 PRINT "1 YOUNGS MODULUS"
2120 PRINT "2 LOW DENSITY"
2130 PRINT "3 HARDNESS"
2140 PRINT "4 PROOF STRESS"
2150 PRINT "5 UTS"
```

```
2160 PRINT "6 FRACTURE TOUGHNESS"
2170 PRINT "7 FATIGUE STRESS"
2180 PRINT "8 LOW RESISTIVITY"
2190 PRINT "9 IMPACT RT"
2200 PRINT "10 LOW COST"
2210 PRINT "HOW MANY PROPERTIES? ";
2220 INPUT N
2230 IF N>10 OR N<1 THEN 2210
2240 DIM C(N)
2250 PRINT "ENTER ";N;" PROPERTY NUMBERS ";
2260 PRINT "         (DECREASING ORDER OF IMPORTANCE)GGGGG"
2270 FOR I=1 TO N
2280 INPUT C(I)
2290 IF C(I)=10 THEN 2310
2300 GO TO 2320
2310 C(I)=12
2320 NEXT I
2330 DIM V(N)
2340 REM***********************FIND MAXIMUM VALUES
2350 I=1
2360 FOR K=1 TO N
2370 V(K)=A(I,C(K))
2380 IF V(K)<>0 THEN 2420
2390 I=I+1
2400 IF I=F+1 THEN 2710
2410 GO TO 2370
2420 FOR J=I+1 TO F
2430 IF A(J,C(K))<V(K) THEN 2450
2440 V(K)=A(J,C(K))
2450 NEXT J
2460 NEXT K
2470 PAGE
2480 PRINT "PROPERTIES ";
2490 FOR I=1 TO N
2500 PRINT C(I);
2510 NEXT I
2520 PRINT
2530 FOR I=1 TO F
2540 FOR K=1 TO N
2550 IF A(I,C(K))=0 THEN 2690
2560 NEXT K
2570 Q=0
2580 K=1
2590 Q=Q+(N+1-K)*A(I,C(K))/V(K)
2600 K=K+1
2610 IF K<N+1 THEN 2590
2620 Q=Q*200/N/(N+1)
2630 REM TO PRINT PROPERTY AND NAME
2640 RESTORE
2650 FOR J=1 TO I
2660 READ A$
2670 NEXT J
2680 PRINT Q,A$
2690 NEXT I
2700 GO TO 2720
2710 PRINT "INSUFFICIENT PROPERTY DATA"
2720 PRINT "ANOTHER COMBINATION ? (Y OR N)GGGG";
2730 INPUT B$
2740 IF B$="Y" THEN 2090
2750 RESTORE
2760 GO TO 120
3000 REM********************************MAX MIN RANGE
3010 PRINT "SELECT 1 MAXIMUM, 2 MINIMUM, 3 SELECTED RANGE   ";
3020 INPUT S
3030 PRINT
3040 IF S=1 THEN 3240
3050 IF S=2 THEN 3090
3060 IF S=3 THEN 3360
```

```
3070 GO TO 3010
3080 REM**********************************************MINIMUM
3090 I=0
3100 I=I+1
3110 C=B(I)
3120 IF C=0 THEN 3100
3130 FOR J=I+1 TO F
3140 IF B(J)=0 THEN 3180
3150 IF B(J)>C THEN 3180
3160 C=B(J)
3170 Z=J
3180 NEXT J
3190 I=Z
3200 GOSUB 5000
3210 PRINT
3220 GO TO 3520
3230 REM**********************************************MAXIMUM
3240 C=B(1)
3250 Z=1
3260 FOR I=2 TO F
3270 IF B(I)<C THEN 3300
3280 C=B(I)
3290 Z=I
3300 NEXT I
3310 I=Z
3320 GOSUB 5000
3330 PRINT
3340 GO TO 3520
3350 REM **********************************************RANGE
3360 PAGE
3370 PRINT "ENTER MAX AND MIN VALUES    GGGGG";
3380 INPUT E,D
3390 PRINT
3400 FOR I=1 TO F
3410 IF B(I)=0 THEN 3500
3420 IF B(I)>E THEN 3500
3430 IF B(I)<D THEN 3500
3440 C=B(I)
3450 GOSUB 5000
3460 IF I<>30 AND I<>60 THEN 3500
3470 PRINT "PRESS RETURN TO CONTNUE"
3480 INPUT A$
3490 PAGE
3500 NEXT I
3510 PRINT
3520 PRINT "PRESS RETURN TO CONTINUE GGGGGG"
3530 INPUT A$
3540 PAGE
3550 GO TO 1010
3560 REM*********************STOP ROUTINE
3570 PRINT @32,18:0
3580 END
4000 REM***************SUBROUTINE TO PRINT TABLE OF MATERIALS
4010 PAGE
4020 RESTORE
4030 FOR I=1 TO F
4040 READ A$
4050 PRINT I;"   ";A$
4060 NEXT I
4070 PRINT
4080 IF P=16 THEN 4130
4090 PRINT "PRESS RETURN TO CONTINUE GGGG"
4100 INPUT B$
4110 RETURN
4120 REM*********************PROPERTIES OF ONE MATERIAL
4130 PRINT
4140 PRINT "ENTER NUMBER OF REQUIRED MATERIAL GGGG";
4150 INPUT I
```

```
4160 RESTORE
4170 FOR J=1 TO I
4180 READ A$
4190 NEXT J
4200 PAGE
4210 PRINT A$
4220 FOR K=1 TO 12
4230 IMAGE 2D,5D.2D
4240 PRINT USING 4230:K,A(I,K)
4250 NEXT K
4260 PRINT
4270 PRINT "PRESS RETURN TO CONTINUE GGGG"
4280 INPUT B$
4290 RETURN
```

```
5000 REM**********************PRINT NAME
5010 RESTORE
5020 FOR J=1 TO I
5030 READ A$
5040 NEXT J
5050 PRINT C,A$
5060 RETURN
```

Program notes

(1) *Reading the data*   The computer used to write this program cannot handle string arrays. The great majority of more modern computers can, but the modifications required are quite minor and will be described at the end of the chapter. The inability to handle string arrays leads to a slight additional content to the program, but not substantial. Rather than use a separate data file which has to be read on each occasion the program is used, and which would mean that the program as printed would be immediately usable on only a limited number of computers since their file handling characteristics all differ substantially, it was decided to include all the names and properties of the selected materials in data statements, and the first block of program lines cover the input data in this form. Lines 800–890 set up the numerical arrays and read the data into them. Line 900 leads on to the next part of the program and line 910 branches to a sub-routine to be described later which prints a list of all the materials covered by the particular selection. The total number of materials stored in the data statements is noted as the variable F in line 130.

(2) *Selection of property*   Lines 1000–1200 list the possible operations that the program can undertake. First, all the materials can be listed, a series of direct properties can be selected by the numbers 1–10, a series of indirect properties can be selected by the serial numbers 11–15, number 16 enables all the properties of one selected material to be printed, number 17 selects the order of merit com-

parison of the materials based on a specified number of selected properties and number 18 stops the program operation. Having selected the required number, lines 1230–1310 branch to the correct part of the program. Lines 1320–1360 construct an array B(I) which contains the property data for the particular property selected for all the materials included in the program. Lines 1370–1440 calculate the array B(I) for the derived property of cost per unit strength. In this case one must reject any material that has a zero entered under the strength property, as the computer cannot handle divisions by zero, and line 1390 accomplishes this. Line 1400 assigns a value of zero to B(I) and this will register as a no property when the selection is made later on in the program. Lines 1450–1730 treat the other derived properties in a similar way.

(3) *Maximum, minimum and range* Having selected the properties that are to be compared, the program now moves to line 3000 and the operator is asked whether it is the material with the maximum or minimum property that is required, or those materials whose properties fall within a selected range. The maximum value of B(I) is selected by lines 3230–3340, where one reads the first property in line 3240 then compares that with every succeeding value of B(I) replacing it if the new value is greater than the original value assigned. This is a simple process and the variable Z is used to count the value of I for which B(I) is a maximum. In principle, selection of the minimum value of B(I) is equally simple, but as some of the values of B(I) are 0, indicating no information, these have to be excluded from the selection process. Lines 3080–3120 read the first non-zero value of B(I). Lines 3130–3180 replace that value with any lower value of B(I) that is not zero. Line 3140 eliminates the values of B(I) that are zero. The sub-routine at line 5000 simply prints the value of C and the name of the material concerned. The name of the material is selected from the data statement by reading the names of the materials until the Ith is reached and printing that name. If the computer handled string variables one would simply print A$(I). Lines 3350–3550 select all those materials whose values lie within specified limits. The limits are entered at line 3380 and then line 3410 eliminates those materials for which there is no information. Lines 3420 and 3430 eliminate those materials that lie outside the specified range. The sub-routine 5000 then prints the value of the property, and lines 3460–3490 enable the screen to be filled with results and cleared before the next set are printed. The sub-routine starting at line 4000 is used both to list the names of the materials considered and also to print the properties of one selected material. As written it does not make use of a string array, but it could simply be modified to do so. Lines 4000–4070 read and print the names of the materials. If it is required to print the properties of one given

material, the program is progressed to line 4130 when the number of the required material is entered and lines 4170–4250 print the name of that material and its list of 12 properties.

(4) *Order of merit rating*   Lines 2000–2760 contain the program for comparing the whole list of materials based on a selection of material properties. The list of properties is given on lines 2100–2200 and it will be noticed that low density, low cost and low resistivity feature in that list. In order to accommodate this inversion of the normal requirement for high properties, the data on each of the materials is inverted in lines 2010–2080. The operator can select at line 2250 how many properties are to be covered. The order of merit rating gives greatest precedence to the first in the list, the next greatest to the second and so on to the last. As stated in Section 6.2, if three properties are specified the first counts as three units, the second property two units and the third property only one unit. If five properties were chosen, then the weighting would be 5,4,3,2 and 1. Having entered the number of properties that are required and having specified those properties, two further arrays $C(N)$ and $V(N)$ are used in the calculation. $C(N)$ is the array of numbers in the list starting at line 2110 which identifies specific properties. The values for this array are entered at 2280. In order to make the calculation, the maximum value for the given property of any of the materials that are included, must be found. These maximum values constitute the array $V(N)$ and the values of $V(N)$ are found in lines 2350–2460. Lines 2380–2410 reject those materials for which no information about the particular property is available and if there is no information for any of the materials then the program transfers to line 2710 where the fact is indicated in a print statement. Having found the maximum value for each of the selected properties possessed by any of the materials in the list, a calculation of the order of merit is made on lines 2530–2620. Each term is taken in sequence and the value of the property $A(I,C(K))$ is divided by the maximum value of that property $V(K)$ and multiplied by the correct weighting factor. Then, at 2620 the order of merit is multiplied by 100 to bring it to a percentage value and divided by the sum of all the weighting factors as indicated earlier in the chapter. The heading for the table of results is printed at lines 2480–2510 and the order of merit and name for each material for which sufficient data are stored and printed at lines 2630–2690. Finally the operator is asked whether another combination of properties is required, if so, the sequence moves to lines 2090 and at 2100 the variables C and V are deleted so that new values can be entered for them at 2280 and 2370. If no further combinations are required then RESTORE at 2750 sets the pointer back to the beginning of the READ statement and

the sequence moves to line 120 where all the data are read in the correct, rather than the inverted form, which has been used in this section of the program.

(5) *Modifications for string arrays*   Only slight modifications are required for a computer that will accept string arrays. In line 500 the string array must be dimensioned and line 830 should be READ A$(I). Line 2680 should read PRINT Q, A$(I) and the previous four lines can be deleted. Line 4050 should read PRINT I;" ";A$(I) and the previous three lines and line 4060 can be deleted. Line 4210 should read PRINT A$(I) and lines 4160 to 4190 can be deleted. Line 5050 should read PRINT C, A$(I) and the previous four lines can be deleted.

PROBLEMS

(6.1) Consider the selection of a material for an overhead electric power line. The properties that will obviously be important are low electrical resistivity, high strength, low density and low cost. Use the program in as many ways as possible to select suitable materials. It will be found that low resistivity favours the choice of copper and a combination of low resistivity and low density favours aluminium and its alloys. The cost per unit of strength favours the steels while the combination of high strength and low resistivity brings in copper and its alloys. Such conductors are actually made of high strength high conductivity copper alloys or of composite steel and aluminium. The various selection criteria built into the program enable these selections to be understood.

(6.2) It may well be of considerable value to be able to print out the contents of the data statements in a clear format to produce a table of all materials and each of their twelve direct properties. Write an element of program that allows this to be done.

(6.3) As written, the program lists the materials in the order that they appear in the data statements. It is interesting to see how much extra complexity would be involved in lines 3350 to 3550 to enable the materials to be listed in decreasing order of value of the specified property. Selection of the maximum value could be done as in lines 3230 to 3340, the value printed, B(I) made zero and the selection of maximum value done a second time and so on. The reader should try to find a way better than this to produce the required result.

Reference

(1) Alexander, W. O., *Contemporary Physics*, **8**, 5, (1967).

Bibliography

Bandrup, J. and Immergut, E. H., *Polymer Handbook*, Wiley, (1975).

Farag, M. M., *Materials and Process Selection*, Applied Science, (1979).

Van Krevelen, D. W., *Properties of Polymers*, Elsevier, (1976).

Index

ABS, 2
Acrylonitrile, 92
Activation energy, 51, 53, 59, 60, 64
Activity, coefficient, 59
  of metal, 59
  of metal ions, 59
Actual strength, 98
Alexander, 124
Alloys, 123
Alloying additions, 53
  element, 58
Alphanumeric characters, 30
Alumina, 50
Aluminium, 30, 49, 50, 105
  alloys, 127
Anelastic, 88
Anelasticity, 80
Arrhenius equation, 51, 59, 64
ASTM grain size, 23, 43, 48
Asymptotic stress, 101
Atomic percent, 18, 33, 45
  positions, 12
  radius, 19
  weights, 18, 34, 45, 92
Aurami, 55
Austenite, 55
AXIS, 9

Bainitic finish temperature, 71
  start temperature, 71
Ball indenter, 117
Barrett, 46
BASIC, 1
Binary eutectic, 21, 36
  diagram, 20
Body-centred atoms, 27
  -cubic, 26, 27, 55, 107
  -tetragonal, 55
Boltzman's constant, 61
Bonding, 77
Brass, 18, 127
Brinell hardness, 105, 118

Brittle fracture, 80
Burgers vector, 15, 16, 44, 103
Burke, 54
Butadiene, 92

Carbon, 65, 77, 92
  content, 58, 70
  fibre expoxide, 128
  fibres, 128
Casting alloys, 123
Cathode, 74
Cell voltages, 74
Centrifugal separation, 93
Ceramics, 93, 128
Characteristic strain, 101
Charpy impact energy, 123, 127
Chlorine, 77
Chromium, 46
Cobalt, 53
Coefficient of work hardening, 103
Composite beam, 115
Composition of a phase, 21
Compound formation, 36
Concentration gradient, 53
Conditional statements, 4
Confidence limit, 23, 43, 47
Considere's construction, 101, 102
Constant pressure, heat capacity, 51
Continuum theory, 104
Cooling rate, 47
Copper, 19, 59, 60, 97, 127
Copper oxide CuO, 59
Coring, 21
Corrosion, 58
COS(X), 2
Cost, 123, 136, 137
  per unit of strength, 124
Covalent compounds, 46
Creep, 123
  resisting alloys, 16
Critical crack size, 124
  resolved shear stress, 99, 106

Cross links, 83
Cross-slip, 97
Crystal planes, 12, 25
  structure, 27

DATA, 3
Data file, 134
  statements, 134
DEF, 7
Defects, 97
Deformation, 97
  of crystals, 25
Degree of polymerization, 77, 84
Dendritic structure, 21
Density, 123, 127, 136, 137
  of packing, 43
Derived properties, 123
Diamond indenter, 117
Diffraction patterns, 13, 25
Diffusion, 21, 52
  coefficient, 53
  profiles, 65
Dilational strain, 29
DIM, 5
Direct properties, 123, 134
Dislocation, 14, 28, 99
  density, 104
  dissociated, 28, 30
  edge, 14, 15, 30
  energy of, 16
  force between, 15
  line, 14, 15
  mobile, 103, 104, 113
  multiplication, 104
  screw, 14, 15, 30
  shear strain surrounding, 29
  strainfield, 15
  velocity, 103, 113
Dissociation pressure, 60
Dynamic hardness, 105

Edge dislocation, 14, 15, 30
Elastic energy, 79, 87
  modulus, 79, 93
  strain, 79, 87, 93
Elastomers, 81, 83, 91, 93
Electric power line, 137
Electrical alloys, 123
  conductivity, 53, 124
  resistivity, 137
Electrochemical cell, 58
Electron/atom ratio, 20
  compounds, 46
  diffraction patterns, 44
  vacancies, 60

Electro-negative elements, 19, 36
Electro-negativity, 19, 36, 46
Electro-positive elements, 19
Elementary alloy theory, 19
Energy of a dislocation, 16
Engineering alloys, 93
  strain, 94, 100, 108
  stress, 94, 100, 108
Enthalpy, 50
Entropy, 50
Equilibrium cooling, 47
  diagrams, 20, 36
Ethylene, 92
Eutectic diagram, 20
  solid, 22, 40
  temperature, 40
EXP, 2

Face-centred, atoms, 27
  -cubic, 27, 55, 97
  crystal, 26
Faraday, 59
Fatigue strength, 23, 127
  stress, 123
Fick's first law, 53
  second law, 53, 65
Flow stress, 99
Flux, 53
Force between, dislocations, 15, 28
FOR...NEXT, 5
Fracture toughness, 127
Free energy, 49

Gaussian error function, 65
Gibbs free energy, 49, 50
Gilman-Johnston, 103
Gold, 19
GOSUB, 6
GO TO, 5
Grain boundary area, 23
Grain size, 22, 58, 70, 127
  dependence, 58
Grain structure, 23, 42, 47
Growth plane, 13

Half-cell potentials, 74
Hardenability, 55, 58, 123
Hardness, 104, 123, 127
  Brinell, 105, 118
  dynamic, 105
  indentation, 105
  Meyer, 106
  Rockwell, 106
  Vickers, 106, 117

Heat capacity, constant volume, 51
    constant pressure, 51
Heat-treatable steels, 123
Hexagonal-close-packed, 55, 97
High-resolution graphics, 30
High-temperature materials, 123
Holes, 60
Holloman relationship, 101
Hooke's law, 98
Hume-Rothery, 18, 34, 46
Hydrogen, 77, 92

Ideal critical diameter, 58
IF. . .THEN, 5
Inclusion content, 23
Indentation hardness, 105
Indirect properties, 134
INPUT, 3
INT, 2
Inter-laminar shear stress, 104, 115
Intermetallic compounds, 46
Internal energy, 50
Interstitial compounds, 46
    solid solutions, 46
Ionic bond, 19

Johnson-Mehl, 54, 67
Johnston-Gilman, 103

Kinetics, 49, 53, 58

Latent heat of fusion, 47
Laves phases, 46
LET, 2
Lever Rule, 21
Liberty ships, 80
Linear elastic fracture mechanics, 124
Liquidus line, 40
LOG, 2
Loops, 5

Martensite, 55
Martensitic finish temperature, 71
    reactions, 55
    start temperature, 71
Materials, 123
Mathematical expressions, 1
Maxwell, 82, 90
McCormick, 84, 96
Mean linear intercept, 23, 42
    molecular weight, 96
    particle size, 24, 43, 48
    surface area per particle, 25
    volume of particle, 25

Mer, 77
    weights, 92
Metallic alloying additions, 55, 70
Metals, 81, 93, 123, 128
Methods of selection, 123
Meyer hardness, 106
Micro-structure, 22, 23, 127
Mild steel, 113, 127
Mobile dislocation, 104
    density, 103, 113
Molecular weight, 77, 84, 85, 92, 128

Negative ion, 19
Nernst equation, 59, 74
Neutral axis, 115
Neutral plane, 104, 105, 115
Nickel based super alloys, 46
Non-equilibrium solidification, 40
Number average molecular weight, 78,
    84, 86
Numerical integration, 96

Order of merit, 123, 125, 134, 136
Overhead electrical conductors, 125
Oxidation, 59, 60
Oxygen, 77, 92

Partial dislocations, 16, 97
Particle distribution, 24
Particles/unit volume, 25
Pauling Electron Valency Number, 46
Peierls-Nabarro stress, 99
Percent, atomic, 33
Phase boundaries, 21, 37, 47
    field, 37
PI, 2
Picture points, 23
Planes, crystal, 12
Plane strain fracture toughness, 123
Plastic deformation, 97
Point defect, 14
Polycrystalline materials, 100
Polymer, 85, 93, 128
    molecules, 77
Polymorphic transformation, 55
Positive ions, 19
Potential, 59
    energy, 51
    of anode, 59
    of cathode, 59
Precipitation hardening, 53, 67
Proof stress, 127
Property data, 126

Primary solubility, 36
    solid solution, 21
PRINT, 4
Program structure, 2
Proof stress, 123
Proportion of the phase, 21
Propylene, 92
P-type semi-conductor, 60

Quantitative metallography, 22, 41

Reaction times, 64
    velocities, 53
READ, 2
Reciprocal lattice, 13
Relaxation time, 81, 88
REM, 7
Resistivity, 123, 136
    data, 67
Restore, 4, 136
RETURN, 7
Rockwell hardness, 106
Rubbers, 128

SCALE, 9
Schmid factor, 99, 107
Screw dislocation, 14, 15, 30
Sedimentation, 93
Self-diffusion, 52, 59, 60
Service temperature, 123
Shape factor, 24, 43
Shear-strain surrounding, dislocation,
    29
Shear stress, 98
    transformations, 55
Sigma phase, 46
Silver, 19
Single crystals, 99
SIN(X), 2
Size factor, 45
Slip, 12, 97, 99
    plane, 13, 107
    systems, 97
Solid solubility, 18, 34
Solidus temperature, 41, 123, 127
Specific modulus, 123
    strength, 123
SQR(X), 2
Stacking fault, 16
    energy, 16, 30, 97
Stacking sequence, 97
Standard deviation, 48
    electrode potential, 59, 74
    001 projection, 30
Steel, 65, 105, 123, 127, 137

Stereographic projection, 17, 30, 32
Strainfield, dislocation, 15
Strains around a dislocation, 28
Strain-hardening coefficient, 101
    exponent, 101
Strain rate, 101
    exponent, 101
Strain relaxation, 80
Strength, 97, 123, 137
    coefficient, 101
Strength of polystyrene, 84
Strengthening mechanisms, 127
Stress sensitivity exponent, 113
Stress-strain curve, 80, 83, 94
String arrays, 134, 137
Styrene, 92
Sub-routines, 6
Subscripted variables, 6
Substitutional solid solutions, 19
Super-cooling, 55
Surface-to-volume ratio, 24, 43

Tektronix computer, 28, 30
Temperature of deformation, 83
Temperatures, solidus, 41
Tensile analysis, 108
    deformation, 100
    elongation, 123, 127
    impact strength, 84, 92
    plastic strain rate, 103
    strength of polystyrene, 96
    tests, 99, 100, 108
Tetragonal structure, 43, 55
Theoretical strength, 97
Thermodynamics, 49, 58
Three-point bending, 104, 115
Tilt boundaries, 16, 44
Time exponent, 54, 67
Titanium alloys, 127
Total cell voltage, 74
Toughness, 80
Transformation kinetics, 54
True strain, 94, 100, 108
    stress, 108
Twinning, 12
Twin plane, 13

Ultimate tensile strength, 127
Unit activity, 59
    cell, 27
    cube, 12, 27
    dislocation, 16
Upper critical temperature, 71
Upper/lower yield, 113

Vacant cation sites, 60
Valency electrons, 19, 36
Vickers hardness, 106
VIEWPORT, 9
Vinylacetate, 92
Vinylchloride, 92
Viscoelastic liquid, 82, 83, 94
   materials, 81
   modulus, 81, 83, 89, 90
   solid, 82, 83, 95
Viscosity, 78
Voce, 101
Voigt, 82, 90
Volume coefficient of compressibility, 51
   coefficient of thermal expansion, 51
   fraction, 24, 43, 48

Weight average molecular weight, 78, 84, 86
   percent, 18, 33, 45
Weighting factors, 126
Width of a dissociated dislocation, 28
WINDOW, 9
Work done in deformation, 80, 87
Work hardening, 103

Yield drop, 103
   point, 103, 113
   strength, 22
Young's modulus, 123, 124, 127

Zinc, 97